"**Immensely helpful.** Generally business owners focus only on the issues at hand and rarely devote time to the issues that can derail their businesses. This book **capsulizes the paths the business owners/leaders need to take to avoid the pitfalls.**"

ASH SUDHAKAR, ESQ., P.E., DEE
CEO and President, Sudhakar Company, Inc.

"Debra Koontz Traverso **makes it easy for a small business to plan for problems.** Everything from disasters to employee/management problems to computer foul-ups and more is covered. Just pick the items that apply to your business, put them together, and there it is—a crisis manual specific to your company."

JAMES N. MORRISON
Director of Governmental Affairs and Emergency Preparedness
Wisconsin Public Service

"Traverso has masterfully taken the lessons learned by large corporations in planning for and responding to crises and put them in **a *practical* how-to guide** that gives the small-business owner all the benefit, but none of the expense, of lessons learned in the field of crisis management. It's **a resource you can put to immediate use** to give you protection...and to give you a good night's sleep."

KEITH H. DINGER
Instructor, Harvard School of Public Health

THE Small Business Owner's Guide TO A Good Night's Sleep

THE Small Business Owner's Guide TO A Good Night's Sleep

PREVENTING AND SOLVING CHRONIC AND COSTLY PROBLEMS

Debra Koontz Traverso

BLOOMBERG PRESS
PRINCETON

Books are available for bulk purchases at special discounts. Special editions or book excerpts can also be created to specifications. For information, please write to: Special Markets Department, Bloomberg Press.

This publication contains the author's opinions and is designed to provide accurate and authoritative information. It is sold with the understanding that the author, publisher, and Bloomberg L.P. are not engaged in rendering legal, accounting, investment-planning, or other professional advice. The reader should seek the services of a qualified professional for such advice; the author, publisher, and Bloomberg L.P. cannot be held responsible for any loss incurred as a result of specific investments or planning decisions made by the reader.

First edition published 2001

1 3 5 7 9 10 8 6 4 2

Library of Congress Cataloging-in-Publication Data

Traverso, Debra Koontz.

The small business owner's guide to a good night's sleep : preventing and solving chronic and costly problems / Debra Koontz Traverso.-- 1st ed.

p. cm.

Includes bibliographical references and index.

ISBN 1-57660-047-5 (alk. paper)

1. Small business--Management. I. Title.

HQ784.T74 T738 2001

658.02'2--dc21   2001025327

ACQUIRED BY **Jared Kieling**

EDITED BY **Maris Williams**

BOOK DESIGN BY **Don Morris Design**

This book is dedicated to three wonderful boys,

all too eager to grow up

and be leaders and heroes in their chosen paths:

my son, Matthew, and my two nephews,

Mark and Joel.

May your future work environments and

professional pursuits be uniquely yours,

filled with satisfaction and success

How to put risks into perspective, protect your assets, identify your vulnerabilities, and prepare your organization for smoldering, as well as unexpected, situations. Not every potential small-business crisis or setback can be addressed in one book, so this chapter helps you prepare a basic response plan for any unexpected situation.

CHAPTER 2

CONDUCT A SMALL BUSINESS SELF-AUDIT 47

You may have problems brewing in your organization and not even know it. This chapter will help you identify where you may be vulnerable and which risks you can eliminate before they become crises or uncontrollable situations.

from financial disaster. This chapter offers a primer to get you started in shopping for the right insurance for your company and situation.

SECTION C

WHEN THE CRISIS MOVES FROM IN-HOUSE TO THE PUBLIC

CHAPTER 7

BRACE YOURSELF FOR NEGATIVE PUBLICITY AND PUBLIC SCRUTINY

Your business did nothing wrong, but the public thinks it did. Enter the news media, who sometimes target businesspeople as villains, and the situation goes from bad to worse. This chapter explains what you should do during unexpected news media encounters, questions, interviews, and visits, and how to deal with negative publicity.

ACKNOWLEDGMENTS

THANKS FIRST GO TO GOD, THAT OMNIPOTENT POWER SO MANY people turn to when tragedy strikes but take for granted the rest of the time. May I never forget how blessed my life has been. I'm especially grateful that—in personal as well as business life—even though we can't go back and make a brand-new start, God makes it possible for all of us to start anew at any moment and make a brand-new ending.

Many incredible people have touched my life either personally or professionally and deserve my deepest personal thanks and public recognition. Ironically, I associate all of these people with risks in one form or another. Those who worked with me professionally either taught me how to eliminate risks in business or worked by my side as we learned it together. Those who have touched me personally encouraged me to take more risks and never to downsize my dreams. These people include Mom, Dad, Alan Koontz, Beth Conny, Shane Bowlin, Denise Crouse, Jean Ritchey, Dorothy Garland, Kerry Stanley, Keith Dinger, Jeanne Gerding, Jim Morrison, Cheryl Jenkins, Jerome Barclay, David Edelman, Lynn Robinson, Chuck Dixon, Donald Bagin, Jeanne Sharbuno, Doug Day, Garrie O'Neill, Richard Wilkins, Shelley Fallon, Randy Goldenberg, Connie Hameedi, Dave Seebart, Todd Steffen, Steve Goldman, Stan Wierman, and Jay Traverso.

Thanks also to my agent team, Mike and Pat Snell, and the exceptional staff at Bloomberg: Jared Kieling, Maris Williams, Lisa Goetz, Tracy Tait, Laurie Lohne, Barbara Diez Goldenberg, JoAnne Kanaval, and Mary Macher.

Introduction

AS I PUT THE FINISHING TOUCHES ON THIS BOOK, THE news media reported that an employee wielding a semiautomatic rifle, shotgun, and pistol had opened fire at an Internet company in Wakefield, Massachusetts, killing seven coworkers. Initial reports said that the shooting was "work related" and dealt with taxes, none of which—as I'm sure time will reveal —had much to do with his seven victims. Tragically, the man's grievance with the company—whether it was real or imagined doesn't matter—has resulted in seven devastated families, nearly 240 distraught and grieving employees, management who will forever wonder if the event could have been avoided, and a company floundering in many directions, attempting to recover from the devastation, the negative attention, and the loss of its most valued asset: quality employees.

By the time you read this book, the shock will be history and the tragedy forgotten, except by those

1

whose lives were personally touched. In the interim, smart employers and personnel directors of companies throughout the country will have adopted some new safety initiatives, no doubt trained supervisors to look for signs of employee stress, and perhaps even penned an emergency response procedure or two. But in time, even neighboring companies in the Wakefield area will have relaxed their vigilance and their vow to maintain top-notch safety and security measures. I've seen it happen time and again.

Unfortunately, it generally takes a tragedy or a crisis to provoke companies to make changes in safety routines and initiatives to safeguard valuable assets. It is my hope that this book will encourage you to take those actions at your company *before* they become necessary.

And, admittedly, the book is about more than the loss of human life in the workplace, although I address workplace violence in Chapter 4. The book is also about viruses, floods, fires, computer crashes, customer relations, sexual harassment, lawsuits, and poor cash flow, to name just a few. It's about any situation that takes your focus away from serving your customers and turning a profit—the primary reasons you are in business. In addition to helping you minimize and, in some instances, eliminate business risks, this book includes a primer to help you strengthen your insurance program and provides how-to's for identifying and tackling your most pressing vulnerabilities.

For years I worked as a crisis management consultant, helping companies of all sizes to safeguard their images and prepare for and manage crises. Because I also have an expertise in public relations and marketing, I used to liken selling my crisis services to selling the most intimidating of all consumer products: cemetery plots. Nobody wants to think or talk about these unpleasant realities. They know it's something they should do and intend to do. They know they ought to plan ahead. They know it's just a matter of time ....

Yet people seem to think that death won't come if they don't plan for it. And business managers think that bad things won't happen if they don't think about them. And little wonder: planning for a crisis can be a thankless, time-consuming undertaking; thankless, that is, until it's needed.

That's why I and the folks at Bloomberg have chosen to structure this book differently from any crisis management book that has come before. Those other books are necessary and thorough, elaborating every detail of structuring a team and equipping a facility. But they're not practical for small businesses. What small business, short on time, resources, and cash, is going to spend days or weeks devising a quality response plan for its tomorrows when it's more concerned about keeping its bottom line intact throughout today? And what insight can you get about your organization from learning what went wrong for others, since no two companies are ever alike? For these reasons, we've created this small-business medicine chest full of fast-acting preventive medicine to help you sleep better at night.

This Book: Your On-the-Shelf Medicine Chest

OPEN THE TYPICAL MEDICINE CHEST IN MOST HOMES and you'll find preventive medicines for the most commonly occurring aches and pains. You'll generally find a bottle of colorful tablets for heartburn, another one filled with liquid for diarrhea, one that dispenses drops one at a time for red eyes, and odorous ones designed to ease muscle pains. And, of course, for those times when you just don't know what's happening to you but you do know that you need some relief, you'll find the standard bottle of aspirin.

Section A (Chapters 1 and 2) of this book is your standard bottle of aspirin. You'll find this fundamental planning section useful for those times when your company is feeling threatened, but you don't know what caused it or what to do about it. It's a good all-purpose medicine to consume right now, today, that will help ease your pains later, leaving you free to concentrate on what you should do to combat the illness once it's been identified.

Section B (Chapters 3 through 6) offers medicines for the most commonly occurring aches and pains and illnesses that plague small businesses. These medicines cover the gamut of necessary treatments: crisis planning, risk communication, damage control, prudent management, insurance coverage, creative negotiation, practical heads-up guidance, survival techniques for attacks and distortions, and even steps designed to save you time. Why the latter? Because for some small businesses, even a computer crash during a tight deadline for an important client can be a near tragedy.

Section C (Chapter 7) deals with the secondary problems with which you would deal should your crisis go public. This information deserves its own chapter, because the response and the reaction by the public to the crisis often becomes bigger than the crisis itself. Exxon learned this the hard way following the *Valdez* incident.

Why This Book Is Necessary

YOUR SMALL BUSINESS'S ADVANCE PREPARATION FOR any type of crisis is more crucial today than ever. Why? You have more competition, and technology has enabled bad news to travel farther, faster, and in various forms ... yes, especially on the Internet. In a time when the words *scam, threat, attack, hidden agenda, injustice, rumor,* and *hacker* have become commonplace along with *computer* and *modem* in the average small business, it's more important than ever to have a plan for negative and unexpected events. Responding fully and truthfully is the only way to stay in good graces with the public you serve. So the next time you feel a small-business headache coming on, reach for this medicine chest and find the right treatment, so that you can restore health to your business as quickly and painlessly as possible and return to getting a good night's sleep.

Principles
of Planning
for a
Small
Business

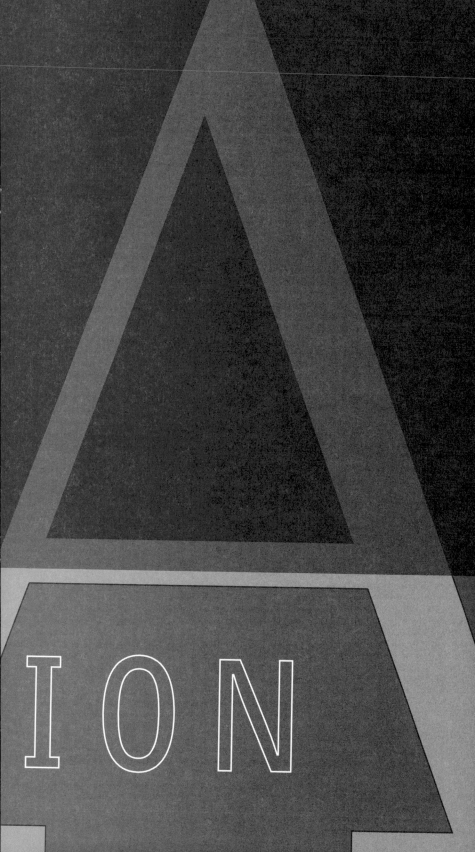

CHAPTER 1

Get Control of Risky Business

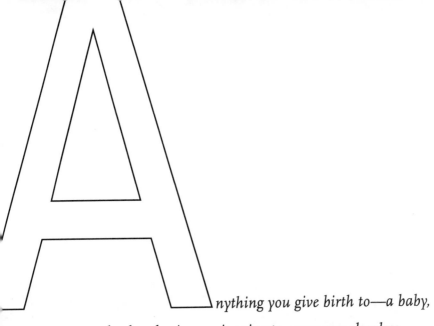

nything you give birth to—a baby, a book, a business—is going to cause you sleepless nights if you haven't safeguarded it against what the world will throw at it. Conversely, if you fortify it with the armor you intuitively and intellectually know it needs, then you'll not only decrease the risks of harm, but you'll increase its opportunities for growth as well.

— LYNN ROBINSON

Owner of Intuitive Consulting for Business and author of *Divine Intuition*

BUSINESS CRISES—THEY'RE IN THE NEWS EVERY DAY. We've all heard about tainted or flawed products, employees who embezzle companies into bankruptcy, and dot-coms that fall from the high-tech wave. But thinking that these crises hit only large companies is as mistaken as thinking that people die only in plane crashes. Sure, it's the big calamities we hear about. However, people are experiencing individual car accidents throughout the country even as you read this sentence. Simultaneously, small businesses are crashing: burning, floundering, failing, declaring bankruptcy, and closing doors in unpublicized silence every day. Further, a U.S. Small Business Administration (SBA) report, "Financial Difficulties of Small Businesses and Reasons for Their Failure," affirms that "the business bankruptcy process is dominated by small businesses."

We don't hear as much about small businesses in trouble for two reasons:

1 Few small businesses have universal—or even nationwide—appeal. Except for politicians and local governments, which survive on their tax base, the perils of a small business are important only to the people who rely on it.

2 It would be impossible to talk about every small

business that experiences a crisis. According to the SBA, the number of business tax returns filed in the United States in 1998 and 1999 was more than 25 million. More than 99 percent were filed by firms defined as "small" by the SBA. It would be impossible to know how many of these businesses experience a serious setback each year, because many are able to continue operating following a crisis, although the day-to-day routine may be forced to shift from "business as usual" to "business as modified." We do know, however (thanks to Dun and Bradstreet statistics as reported to the SBA), that more than 83,000 small businesses failed in 1997 (the last year for which statistics are available). It's safe to assume that unwelcome events led to these failures, because the statistic is distinguished from a second category of companies titled "Terminations," wherein voluntary closures were calculated. Another document, entitled "Open for Business" (1999), by the Institute for Business and Home Safety, says that "at least 25 percent of businesses never reopen following a local disaster." Insurance industry surveys find that figure low, however; but then, it's in their best interest to settle on the high end of survey results so that they can entice small businesses to consider buying more coverage. The number they use, industrywide, is generally between 43 and 45 percent.

Given any of these statistics, the important question to ask is no longer "Should small businesses plan for a crisis?" but rather "For what kinds of crises should small businesses plan?" and "How do they go about it?" The answers to both questions dictated the content of this book—you will learn how to avoid or overcome the top setbacks and crises that small businesses face. Of course, there are situations other than those described in this book that can inflict harm on your small business, situations that arise as a result of circumstances specific to the unique nature of your business or industry. For these, you'll read steps you can take to fortify your company against any unexpected situation when it occurs.

When you read "*any* unexpected situation" in the previous sentence, note that this is not hype or exaggeration. Your goal should be to fortify your business against all potential perils so that you are free to concentrate on turning a profit. Therefore, *any* situation that takes your focus away from your primary reason for being in business is a hindrance to growth, and perhaps even to survival. Even a brief snowstorm can keep your customers and employees away. A fire at your supplier's offices may be the supplier's crisis, but it's still your problem if you're waiting on a delivery that may never come. And your employees do more than work for a living, or even more than work while they're at work (look to Linda Tripp and Monica Lewinsky for proof). Good management, then, dictates that you eliminate as much risk as you can. Chapter 2 will show you how to conduct an audit to identify potential problems, so that you can eliminate as much risk as possible. For the risks you can't eliminate, it's wise to organize a plan now so that you will deal successfully with the unexpected when it does occur.

Preparing a business plan and practicing quality management are good starts, but they are not enough to assure that your business will have the chance to grow. Usually trouble is not caused by a flaw in your business plan. Rather, it comes from other factors, such as the employees you take on, the fickleness of the marketplace, updates in technology, or changes in societal practices, making consumers' demand for products shift focus. IBM, for example, once had a virtual monopoly on the computer business, but changes in societal demands, along with deficient forward planning, have caused it to face many business problems in recent years.

Thinking about the unlikely is actually a productive use of your time and should be a part of any business strategy. Answering the question "Where is my company vulnerable?" can identify deficiencies and lead to strategic thinking and creative ways of doing business. Recognizing and planning to deal with potential setbacks—including everything from time wasters to crises—should be a part of up-front planning rather than reactionary crisis management later on, when your efforts might prove too late or too little to do much good. Preparing plans now lets you realize your vulnerabilities in a safe, controllable environment rather than in front of clients, backers, neighbors, or even a jury.

Understanding and Preparing for Risks

THIS BOOK STRESSES THE NEED FOR FUTURE-ORIENTED EVENT management, for objective assessment of operations and processes, for development of problem-solving skills, for enough security to protect your assets, and for the ability to distinguish between perception and reality when it comes to your customers and the news media.

Since your company is unlike any other, there is no one-size-fits-all method by which to address the unexpected situations that are going to come your way. The definition of a time waster, a setback, or a crisis will differ from one company to another, even within the same industry. So this book is designed to build recognition that negative things do happen, to help you change what you can now, and to leave you prepared for the most predictable of business problems: the unpredictable.

RISKY BUSINESS

FOR PURPOSES OF THIS BOOK, A RISK IS DEFINED AS ANY-thing that threatens the plans you have made for your business, from simple but annoying time wasters to major destructive crises. In the end, or perhaps even immediately, a risk to a small business can result in a substantial financial loss. If you were a major corporation, you'd have a risk management department to plan for the perils of growing a company, launching a new product, entering a new market, or taking on more employees. Instead, you're small, but with this book you're also equipped to cope. Even if you have several years of successful operation to your credit, it's still wise to plan for the unexpected, because what has or has not happened in the past is not an appropriate indicator of the future.

For example, no doubt none of the following situations have ever happened to your business, but perhaps they could. They each have happened to other businesses, and for each of those businesses, the situation was completely unexpected.

Do you know how you would respond? Do your employees know what they should do? Do you know whom to call and how to call them? Do you know how to deal with angry customers and curious news media if they ask questions?

◆ A workplace assault involving a disgruntled or former employee

◆ A whistle-blower steps forward and says that drug use, theft, racial discrimination, sexual harassment, or criminal misconduct is occurring at your company—even though it is not.

◆ A suicide on your premises

◆ A violent domestic squabble on your property

◆ A small fire that destroys your computer equipment and/or your inventory

◆ A call from the police saying that one of your company vehicles was involved in an accident, that your driver was at fault, and that two children were killed

◆ A media inquiry into the safety of your product because an anonymous user claims the product is tainted

◆ A spill of hazardous materials right outside your office door, calling for the evacuation of residents in the area. When video footage of the spill is shown on the news that night, the reporter announces that it occurred outside your company offices, implying that you're somehow associated with the problem.

◆ A computer crash in the midst of rushing to meet a very lucrative client's deadline

PUTTING YOUR RISKS INTO PERSPECTIVE

IT MAY SEEM INAPPROPRIATE TO ATTRIBUTE TO "MERE" TIME wasters the same damaging potential we attribute to destructive crises. However, having owned two small businesses and seen how precious time is to an understaffed operation, I know that time wasters can wreak as much havoc on a bottom line as a major fire or creditor dispute. Although the National Federation of Independent Business reports that the estimated cost for a business owner's defense in the average lawsuit is a whopping $100,000, the biggest drain to the business could be the hundreds of hours expended by the owner in dealing with the case. And downtime due to computer failure or data loss may be many entrepreneurs' worst nightmare, yet Ontrack Data International, a Minnesota-based data recovery service, estimates that fewer than 40 percent of entrepreneurs back up their data at least once a week. So data loss poses a considerable risk for 60 percent of all small businesses. An unexpected situation doesn't have to be life-and-death to be a serious threat to you.

Addressing risks before they become mistakes, regrets, and crises will automatically strengthen your management practices; therefore, this book is as much about perfecting your day-to-day management as it is about preparing for tomorrow's unexpected events. For example, your management practices may involve serving your biggest customer with almost all of your time. That may seem like a great strategy, since this person is the one providing all your income. But if you lose that company for some reason, you will go from positive to zero income overnight.

That happened to Charlie McGovern, owner of a small engineering consulting firm in Gaithersburg, Maryland. McGovern advises, "Never depend on a single customer or contract. I relied upon one corporate customer to keep us fully employed for several years. Then their national corporate office decided to start calling the shots at the regional level. Our contract was awarded to someone else. I had to let my two part-time employees go and start over. Bottom line is, once you get one customer or contract, use it to get more customers. Otherwise your income will be at risk, as will your bargaining position with the single customer."

BREAKING DOWN THE RISKS

ONE STRATEGY OFTEN EMPLOYED IN RISK MANAGEMENT IS TO disaggregate risk. Put simply, this means to take a large, complicated risk and break it down into smaller, more manageable pieces. Let's look at this situation at its most basic level: that of a small business operated in someone's home. The risk? In this case, a married couple is trying to run and build a company together from their home, but their work routines are not compatible. As is well documented, the main roadblocks to working from home are psychological, not technical. Thus, the risk here is for the survival of not only the company but the marriage as well.

Jason and Marilyn Fogle (not their real names) operate a home-based business that advises small companies on strategy, information systems, marketing, and management issues. The problems? One liked to think out loud, the other felt interrupted every time someone spoke. One was a morning person; the other liked to take naps midday despite pressing deadlines. One spoke too loudly on the phone. The other took liberties with office supplies no matter whose desk they came from.

The solution was to lessen the risk that they would eventually dissolve the company or perhaps even get a divorce due to anger and disagreement. To disaggregate their risk, they installed fabric-covered panels in their office to cut down on noise. They set ground rules on talking out loud, because they realized that the interruptions were undermining each other's productivity. They wrote down and accepted established work hours for one another, and they made a vow to take in a matinee movie each week as a diversion to their daily routine.

YOUR RESPONSE CHOICES

WHEN DEALING WITH A RISK THAT THREATENS YOUR COMPANY, you have two reasonable choices:

◆ **Shift the responsibility for it.** Companies have learned to shift the responsibility for a risk by purchasing as much insurance as they can afford. However, according to insurance industry estimates, every $1 of insured loss is accompanied by $3 of uninsured economic loss, such as lost profits and business opportunities.

Often the problem is that owners ask only "Are we insured to cover loss?" What they should also ask is "How will this situation affect our critical business processes? Operations? Services? Personnel? Customers? Deliveries? Facilities? Stock? And all intangible assets such as reputation? Trust? Goodwill? Competitive edge? Employee morale? Work in progress?"

◆ **Eliminate it, accept it, and/or manage it.** The bulk of this book deals with eliminating, accepting, and managing the risks with which the small business owner must deal.

Is it possible and practical for you to identify risks and to plan for the unexpected? Yes, even though you don't have a legal department and PR agencies to call on, and even though you will have to handle unexpected situations yourself, it is easier than you might think to plan ahead. It's a must for survival; after all, your margin of error is smaller than it is for a large corporation. One crisis could put you out of business, whereas for a larger corporation with brand-name recognition and leading market share, the same situation might not be a concern. Larger corporations can generally outlast their critics and crises.

Let's say that you are in a high-tech business and that you produce a product for personal computers. Now suppose someone proves to the news media that your product is defective. This situation happened to Intel Corporation. Intel's handling of its flawed Pentium chip problem was dubbed the "Dumbest Move of 1994" by *Business Week*. Like most companies, Intel's practices and policies were designed to handle day-to-day operation, not unexpected events. As a result, the company wasn't prepared. Sure, it's a $12 billion company, but it had to take almost $500 million as a pretax charge in fourth quarter 1994 to replace or write off the flawed chip. Do you suppose your business could survive as long as Intel did (six months) before it finally admitted that its response was, in the words of Intel CEO Andrew Grove, "arrogant and uncaring"? Intel is the world's largest manufacturer of computer chips, so it survived. Your doors, however, may have long been closed.

YOUR ASSETS ARE WORTH PROTECTING

YOU WILL ALSO WANT TO PREPARE YOURSELF FOR UNEXPECTED situations because you have so many assets to protect. Assets include more than equipment and inventory. Assets are anything owned or that is a part of your company that has value. Below is a list of assets identified by the attendees at one of my planning seminars. You may have even more assets to add to the list. Go through the list item by item and think about the security or precautionary measures you have in place to protect each.

TANGIBLE ASSETS	INTANGIBLE ASSETS
Accounts receivable	Brain trust (the understanding
Cash	your employees have collect-
Cash flow	ed of your business and its
Certifications and licenses	purpose)
Computer data/records	Claims rating
Copyrights	Credibility
Customer database	Employee pride
Customers	Experience
Equipment	Integrity
Facilities	Liabilities
Inventory	Market share
Leasehold interests	Product leadership
Mailing lists	Reputation
Patents	Stockholder confidence
Personnel	
Raw materials	
Suppliers (your relationship,	
contracts with them)	
Trademarks	

WHAT CAN HAPPEN

I HAVE WORKED WITH MANY BUSINESS OWNERS DURING AND after a crisis. By far, their most common mistakes fell into one of these nine categories:

1 Failing to plan
2 Ignoring warning signs
3 Failing to prepare material in advance so that it's on hand when a crisis hits
4 Being overly optimistic that they could "weather a storm"
5 Making decisions too slowly
6 Making decisions based on fear, not facts
7 Failing to communicate with the people who need to know about the situation, such as employees
8 Failing to return phone calls from the news media or using

"guilty" phrases like "No comment"

9 Being unwilling to make changes or adjustments

AS A RESULT, THESE BUSINESS OWNERS EXPERIENCED THE following:

◆ A damaged reputation that eventually lead to closing doors
◆ Loss of employee morale and loyalty, or even complete employee turnover
◆ A decrease in production because the focus shifted from "business as usual" to survival
◆ Fewer sales and reduced profits
◆ Expensive name changes in an attempt to create a new identity
◆ Hefty attorney fees—Not having documentation to show preplanning has brought charges of negligence and legal liability to many business owners when something adverse happened to an employee or visitor. Having something in writing shows that the owner made an effort to protect people.
◆ Crippling fines

IN CONTRAST, LET'S LOOK AT WHAT RESULTED FOR BUSINESS owners who experienced the unexpected but had planned ahead through their day-to-day management structure:

◆ Extended visibility
◆ Heightened customer awareness and understanding of the business
◆ Increased name recognition
◆ Stronger bonds with people and groups important to the business's success
◆ Improved reputation and credibility
◆ Validated management plans
◆ Enhanced confidence for the business owner

A COMPANY THAT LEARNED THE HARD WAY

ASK THE OWNERS OF ATLANTA-BASED BLOOMING COOKIES Catalog Company the importance of thinking "What-if?" Ann King and Ashley Ghegan today run a $4 million business, but they experienced unexpected negative situations in their start-up and growth years that would have put many entrepreneurs out of business. Included among these missteps were inexperience, a string of not-so-strategic alliances, misleading real estate agents and landlords, poor location, employee betrayal, arson, lack of training in how to talk to the news media, inadequate insurance, poor advice from bankers and loan officers, and a lack of safeguards for proprietary information.

Did each of these situations really cost them that much in time and money? Yes. Let's look at just one: poor location. Early in her business, King signed a three-year lease for a 500-square-foot space tucked away in a small shopping center. She recalls that her real estate agent "calmed my concerns about my new location by saying, 'Don't worry about the lease. If you're not successful, we'll let you out of it, because we don't want you here if you're not doing well.'" Not only did the roof leak, but also "you could have shot a cannon through the shopping center at any time of the day and not even come close to hitting anybody. There was no traffic. I learned the hard way that you don't go into a shopping center unless it has an anchor, like a grocery store, to bring in traffic. We were virtually off the customer radar map that year. That unexpected turn of events cost us thousands and thousands of dollars." Indeed, King says her sales dropped almost 35 percent. "If I had not done mailings, I'm not sure we would have stayed in business." How to make sure you've identified a good location and other tips for the adverse situations King experienced are discussed in Chapters 2, 3, 4, and 7.

START BY MAKING A LIST

KING'S SITUATION PROVES THAT YOU DON'T HAVE TO SPLIT atoms at a commercial nuclear power plant to experience highly damaging situations. If you produce a product, you could be the victim of sabotage or product tampering. Moreover, if you operate a service company, you could be oblivious to the exact nature of the storm over the horizon. However, with a little thought and discussion with employees, you could probably develop a long list of scenarios that could happen to your company. The box on pages 24–25 offers a

Potential Crisis Situations

Technological accidents

- air and space disasters
- air quality problem
- chemical release
- chemical spill
- computer problems
- contaminated product
- EPA shutdown of facility
- equipment failure
- explosion
- fire
- gas leak
- government probes or fines
- hazardous by-products
- medical problems
- offices made unavailable
- power failure
- process failure
- radiation accident
- transportation accident

Natural disasters

- avalanche
- contamination
- dam failure
- drought
- earthquake
- extended severe cold
- famine
- fire
- flood
- heat wave
- hurricane
- ice storm
- infestation
- insect infestation
- landslide
- lightning
- meteorological hazard
- sinkhole
- snowfall
- severe storm
- tornado
- volcano
- wild animals

Internal concerns

- class-action lawsuits
- computer virus
- consumerism actions
- corporate takeover
- damaging rumors
- discrimination or harassment charges or claims
- economic downturn
- embezzlement
- employee layoff or downsizing
- executive deaths
- executive dismissals
- loss of significant business from one or more customers
- major promotional error
- media scare (real or not)
- mismanagement
- on-the-job incidents

- poor financial performance
- product problem or recall
- scandal
- shareholder suit
- strike, lockout, picket, or boycott
- supplier disaster
- violent threats or actions by a disgruntled current or former employee
- whistle-blowing
- workplace violence

External threats and other hazards
- bomb threat
- communication failure
- crisis in same industry
- crisis at neighbor
- crisis thought to be yours
- government restriction
- hostage situation
- kidnapping
- legislation
- no property access
- rumors being spread
- sabotage, theft, or arson
- someone else's crisis on your property
- supplier loss
- terrorist threat
- transportation loss

Anticipatory events
- executive departure
- executive resignation
- executive incapacity
- fraud discovered
- key customer loss
- key supplier loss or failure
- poor earnings expected
- power to be shut off
- construction, remodeling
- serious product problem discovered
- severe weather or storm forecast

External threats due to your location
- airport
- chemical plant
- federal building
- foreign embassy
- hazardous neighbor
- landfill
- major highway
- major railway
- military base
- nuclear power plant
- ocean
- office above tenth floor
- river's floodplain

list of potential crisis situations you will want to review. Since disasters don't always work the 9-to-5 shift, I've included a wide variety of unexpected events to get you thinking about all sorts of hours, weather conditions, people issues, market fluctuations, and more.

Where Is Your Company Vulnerable?

THE IDEA IS TO IDENTIFY YOUR VULNERABILITIES AND YOUR areas of risk, then prevent them from turning into crises. Once you've identified your vulnerabilities, ask yourself if there's anything you can do now to prevent them from turning into problems or crises. For each vulnerability, list the actions you intend to take to eliminate or lessen the risk of it becoming a crisis.

As you go through the list, keep in mind that the predictability of a threat and the frequency of a threat help to determine the probability of its occurrence. Your analysis should also include realistically examining your current preventive measures that will minimize the probability that these negative situations occur.

Employees sometimes are in a much better position to spot problems and to be objective about those problems than the owner of the company is. For that reason, involve your employees in identifying potential problems. Have them fill out a Vulnerability Assessment as described at the end of this chapter. Also, walk through Chapter 2 with your employees. Together, you can eliminate some situations that—if left unattended—could escalate into severe problems someday.

QUALITY MANAGEMENT ALONE ISN'T ENOUGH

BUSY ENTREPRENEURS OFTEN ASK WHETHER PREPLANNING for unexpected situations is really necessary. After all, they pride themselves in practicing quality management on a day-to-day basis. Unfortunately, quality management practices do not preclude a company from being drawn into a crisis; just ask Nebraska-based Bluebird Nursery, which experienced a devastating flood, or the Blue Coat Inn in Dover, Delaware, which was destroyed by fire. Or ask the Alabama-based manufacturing firm Dorsey Trailers, Inc., which needed to borrow $25 million to recover when a levee on the nearby Pea River gave way. (You'll read more about these incidents in Chapter 2.) Sure, quality management may help you avoid problems in the first place, but general management principles do not dictate that you conduct a fact-finding mission in which you go looking for trouble. Yet that's exactly what you should do: find the trouble spots before they find you—that's prudent management, the kind of management that bankers, investors, and lending institutions look for. And find the help you'll need prior to needing it. To use a universal example that most people can relate to: The time to find the flashlights and the candles to illuminate your space during a power outage is not after the electricity goes out but rather before, when you have no reason to believe that it will ever go out.

No matter how strong a company's management techniques are, a crisis can still occur. Some events, such as product tampering, hostile takeovers, or natural disasters, may not be preventable, but that fact does not exempt a company from living with the consequences. The response to these crises is within the company's control, and it has to take some ownership of the problem.

Look at one of the most well-known business crises in history: Johnson and Johnson's Tylenol tragedy. In 1982, the company experienced a tampering horror in which seven people in the Chicago area died from consuming cyanide-laced capsules. J&J recalled more than 31 million bottles and watched its share of the analgesic market plunge from more than 35 percent to less than 7 percent. And, J&J will tell you, it had practiced quality management prior to the scare. Fortunately, its quality management included planning for the unexpected—a broad recall. J&J already had communication links, a response network, and an awareness of how it wanted to be perceived when the public relations damage was done, so it responded accordingly.

In the end, after the crisis is past—and sometimes even while it is still unfolding—you may be quizzed about how diligent you were in your efforts to identify potential problems and then initiate changes or offer solutions. Who will quiz you? Angry employees, disgruntled customers, hungry attorneys, excited news media, and, if you have them, anxious stockholders.

CREATE A PLAN OF ACTION

IF YOU IMMEDIATELY PICTURE A PLAN AS ONE OF THOSE VOL-uminous binders sporting dozens of tabs that employees at large organizations keep displayed on their shelves, then you've got the wrong idea of what I mean when I say you need a plan. Sure, those programs are necessary, and they work for those organizations. And I'm proud to say that I'm one of those specialists who has helped dozens of large corporations prepare for crises through the use of such programs. But since your company is small and has fewer resources, you don't necessarily need an extensive program encased in a binder. What you need is a plan of action. This plan could take many forms, depending upon the size and focus of your company. It could spell out each task assigned to each member of a "crisis" team that assembles in a "war" room when an emergency is declared. This is ideal if you have enough employees and a facility to support such an investment in planning. However, if you're like most small businesses that are limited in resources, your plan may consist of simple checklists of action steps to take regardless of the type of crisis. The point is to do what you can, and as much as you can, before it's too late to do anything. A small investment of time can go a long way in averting damage to your business.

First, look at the vulnerability identification work sheets you completed with your employees, as described earlier in the chapter. Take a look at the list of action steps you and your employees outlined and determine which ones can be done in advance so you can be better prepared if the unexpected occurs. You may find that what's left to be done at the time the unexpected hits is the same from one sheet to another. Thus, you have the beginnings of your simple plan. It will prove particularly valuable during the first few hours of an emergency, when you may not know what to do or what's really happened. Your plan can serve as an invaluable road map during a stressful time when strategic thinking can give way to rash decision making. If you want to go that extra step—and it may be possible, depending on the size of your staff—then list who is responsible for each action that should be taken. Remember, though, the plan you develop is a living document, meaning that as you grow, change employees, move location, and diversify, your plan must reflect those changes. Because employee turnover is so high in many small businesses, make it a practice to review the crisis plan at least every three months.

QUESTIONS TO ASK

AS YOU DEVELOP YOUR PLAN OF ACTION, ASK YOURSELF:

♦ **Who will respond?** Does the plan identify everyone involved who will respond to the emergency, and who will be in charge? It's important to designate one decision maker or coordinator who can make educated decisions. Will it be the same person if the situation were to occur at 2 A.M. instead of 2 P.M.? Will everyone know this? Is there at least one backup (two is even better) in case the primary person is out of town? And assuming no coordinators show up, are other staff members trained in what steps to take, and do they have the authority to do so? I once worked with a small company near Cleveland that organized a response team of about twenty-five people. To test the amount of time it would take to get everyone together during nonwork hours, the owner factored in the amount of time it would take each employee to arrive from home, then assigned a coordination role to the two people living nearest to the company offices. It seemed like a great plan until an emergency hit on a Saturday afternoon. The first designated coordinator was out of town, and the second one refused to come in because he was home alone with the kids and couldn't contact his wife, who was out running errands.

♦ **How can responders be reached?** Does the plan include an updated, thorough, easy-to-follow telephone directory with home numbers of employees, current numbers of local responding agencies (i.e., fire, police), and numbers for those supplies and services that may be needed (i.e., Who will feed everyone at 3 A.M.? Who will fix a broken fax machine or emergency vehicle on Christmas Day?). Having these lists in your office, or wherever you decide to assemble during a crisis, is generally adequate. However, one list you will want to make available at all times is that of employees' telephone numbers, including cell phones and beepers. The best way to ensure that employees have emergency numbers available at all times is to create an abbreviated list, reduce it on a photocopy machine (or create it in very small text on the computer) until it's the size of a credit card, laminate it, and request that all employees keep it in their wallets. Give them a second one to keep in the glove compartment of their cars.

◆ **Where will responders meet?** Does the plan establish policies for obtaining and using facilities, equipment, services, and other resources required for any emergency situation, in case something happens when the owner is out of town? You may have to get creative if you have a small office. Does a neighboring facility have a larger office you could borrow during an emergency? They might even have an auditorium you could use in case the news media arrive in large numbers. Hotels, conference centers, and libraries generally have meeting rooms, too. If you're just going to rely on your office, determine whether it has enough phones to handle the increased number of phone calls you may need to make and receive.

◆ **How will responders know what to do?** Does the plan demand periodic training for responding personnel? Do they understand how they are supposed to respond? Do they know what their duties are? Do they understand the duties of other employees with whom they must interact? Do they know who can make decisions or who to turn to for guidance? Do they know what parts of your business need to be up and running as soon as possible? Do they know not to talk to the media? To curious observers or callers? Do they know how to operate necessary emergency equipment? Do they know to take detailed notes of every action and phone call? At a minimum, you will want to make sure that time is not lost to duplication of efforts and that all vital steps on your checklist are carried out. Walking through a plan in advance, and on a regular basis, can ensure all steps are addressed.

- **Will responders understand the magnitude of the situation?** Does the plan offer guidance on what constitutes the need to refer to the plan of action? An explosion? Angry phone calls? Involving employees in your planning generally addresses this situation, since it would be impossible to list every crisis that may hit. When you involve employees in the planning, they will get a sense of what the company's greatest threats are and how they should be handled. For example, in addition to losing revenue during a crisis, you may face contractual fines or penalties if you cannot meet your obligations. If your employees are involved in planning, they will get a better sense of the company's responsibilities and contractual agreements.

- **Will we be able to continue operations?** Does the plan make provisions for handling an adverse situation while simultaneously carrying out the normal operations of the business? If routine matters are ignored, will that too develop into a crisis? After all, the crisis may rob you of time and attention, but it may not affect your ability to continue day-to-day operations. If you can continue business while you deal with the crisis, then do so. This may involve bringing in some temporary staff or seeking outside counsel. It's best not to divide attention, however, so if you can, separate any employees who are working on the crisis from those who are handling the day-to-day issues. Continued operations could also rely on external resources: If your usual supplier is forced to shut down due to a crisis, you will wish that you had made an occasional purchase with a supplier outside of your local area. So do it now for uninterrupted operations down the road.

- **How will we handle the news media?** Does the plan provide resources for answering news media calls? Are background and educational materials ready now to distribute at the time of an emergency? Many of the questions you will receive from the news media during adverse times can be answered now, simply by preparing fact sheets about your company. For example, reporters are likely to ask: What service/product do you provide? How large is your staff? What is the mission of your company? Who are your chief customers? Who are your suppliers? How do you carry out your services? How are your products made? All these questions can be answered in advance on a fact sheet.

◆ **Can we keep the crisis and the response isolated?** Does the plan address security measures? Is the "war room" (command center, tiny office, dining room, wherever the meeting location is for all matters dealing with the event) insulated from leaks and prying eyes of the press? Of course you should always tell the truth in a crisis situation, but you may have to talk about confidential information with employees as you plot your response, and you do have the right to retain the confidentiality of much company intellectual information.

WHAT TO INCLUDE

YOUR PLAN OF ACTION SHOULD INCLUDE INFORMATION ON

◆ **Staff assistance.** List who is responsible for what to avoid duplication of efforts or the possibility that a critical task will go undone.

◆ **Communications.** Include contact information of all key company personnel and critical outside resources. Know how you'll keep employees, customers, and key contacts informed.

◆ **Supplier issues.** Find out what emergency plans your vendors have and whether they're equipped to support you if necessary.

◆ **Data protection.** Develop a data-backup program to assure that critical information won't be lost if you experience a situation such as a fire or flood. (If possible, protect your company with emergency lighting, sprinkler systems, smoke detectors, fire extinguishers, clearly marked utility shutoffs, and backup generators.)

◆ **Security.** Outline how you will keep employees and your facility safe and secure if something happens. Know who has keys to the building, and keep duplicate sets in a secure place both at and away from the office.

◆ **Relocation.** If your facility is rendered inaccessible or unusable, where will you relocate temporary day-to-day operations? Will your crisis response occur from the same location?

Additionally, developing a plan of action does more than remove much of the risk and uncertainty. It can also provide you with more control over your destiny. You may be able—in part—to choose when and where a problem erupts, giving you not only time to prepare but also more ability to control the flow, the speed, the direction, and the duration of the unexpected event. You might also control how quickly you'll recover from the incident. For example, if you can recover from an industrywide crisis faster than your competition, with more of your capabilities intact, your business is more likely to retain its market share and make gains. This also will preserve your employees, along with their skills and knowledge.

SETTING UP A TEAM WHEN YOU'RE UNDERSTAFFED

IF YOUR COMPANY WERE ALREADY A MIRROR REFLECTION OF your dream company, no doubt it would have hundreds of employees to choose from to set up a response team for adverse times. However, you may be a company of just a few dozen or a couple of people. Perhaps just you alone are the response team.

Because every reader of this book has a unique structure and environment to deal with, it would be impossible to answer here how each company should establish a team. Overall, however, the following areas or responsibilities need to be addressed during a crisis. If you're a small staff, then you'll have to double and triple up on responsibilities. Or, consider bringing in outside experts.

◆ **Someone in charge.** This person may also be known as an "emergency director" in larger organizations. If you have staff to choose from, then choose wisely. Don't necessarily put yourself in this position. You may need to oversee continued operations while the crisis is dealt with. Besides, the person who can look at the situation most objectively may not be the person who is in the middle of it all. What you want is someone who can offer fresh action, not frightened reaction. Sometimes someone outside of the response, or even outside of the company—such as a trusted consultant—may be the best selection for this responsibility.

◆ **Coordinator.** This person manages the team and the response facility but not the crisis. This position is only necessary if you have a large response staff.

◆ **Financial coordination.** Unexpected purchases and payments may have to be made during a crisis. Someone has to know what the company can afford to do. If an accountant keeps your books, then talk to him in advance to secure his availability during a crisis.

◆ **Human resources.** Employees will have a lot of concerns and questions during a crisis situation. The last thing you want is for them to learn the details of the crisis from their neighbor or a reporter.

◆ **Marketing.** Someone should review the response steps you're taking to make sure they don't undermine your marketing and advertising efforts. After all, your crisis response is temporary, hopefully, whereas the return to your "normal" routine is what you're striving to achieve. If you must respond in a manner counter to the image you project in your promotional messages, then make sure these messages are suspended indefinitely. You don't want to be caught launching an ad for a product tomorrow that was identified as defective today. If you're too strapped to handle this aspect, call in a public relations firm.

◆ **Technical input.** If your crisis involves receiving information from a location separate from your office, such as a service area or small factory, then how are you going to get that information in an expeditious manner? It may not serve the team well to leave the meeting area to go to the site of the crisis because they will be separated from phones and materials they need to develop an effective response. Therefore, make sure you have a reliable and dedicated liaison or informant at the location from which you need all your answers. Sometimes this situation will involve information that only your supplier has. If so, meet with your representative now to secure the company's willingness to support you during a crisis.

- **Operations.** Changing one aspect of how a small company operates can have severe repercussions on other aspects of the company. Make sure someone with overall operations knowledge is involved in making those changes.
- **Information systems.** You or your response team may need vital company information in the middle of the night. How are you going to get it if the only person familiar with the LAN is unavailable?
- **Facilities.** This is a concern if you have several facilities to safeguard or need to reconfigure current facilities to accommodate your crisis response.
- **Security.** If your office is damaged, how will you secure the salvaged equipment and usable supplies before you are able to move them to your new headquarters?
- **Legal advice.** You should have a trusted attorney that you can call on at all hours of the day.
- **News media.** If the crisis interests them, they may have questions. Lots of questions. They'll assume that you have the answers. If you don't, they'll get answers from someone else. If you don't want someone else talking for your company, such as a competitor or a disgruntled employee, then determine now who will serve as spokesperson.
- **Public relations.** Depending upon the scope of the crisis, your image might be severely tarnished. Someone should determine the public relations repercussions of any actions you take during a crisis.
- **Insurance.** The stipulations in your insurance policy might alter the way you respond to a crisis. Make sure your insurance carrier will be available during a crisis to assist.
- **Clerical support.** If you have administrative support available, let them do the running, copying, and support tasks, while you and your team concentrate on the crisis.

THIS LIST POINTS OUT THE NEED TO LOOK OUTSIDE YOUR organization for help. You may find help from temporary employment agencies, an attorney you can keep on retainer, a public relations firm, your insurance carrier, off-duty police officers or security guards, and/or a trusted consultant. The only catch is that you should line them up now. The time to shake hands for the first time or to explain your company's mission is not in the midst of a crisis or concern but rather when all is calm.

Go through the list on the previous pages and begin to compare your staffing and your situation. Who could handle the news media? Are you the best one to speak for your company? Who has the authority to make important financial decisions? Who can best handle technical glitches? As you're thinking about who (and how many people) you would want to assign to a response team, consider who can best deal with the following frustrating situations. This is a list of elements common to most unanticipated crises *when the company was unprepared,* as identified by other small business owners who've weathered them:

◆ no time to make decisions
◆ no objective source to turn to when making decisions
◆ unanticipated consequences seem to crop up endlessly
◆ getting complete information seems almost impossible
◆ information is wrong, and if it's right, it can't be trusted
◆ you are nervous, thus everyone involved is nervous
◆ because you are small or alone, a sense of being targeted can overwhelm you
◆ an atmosphere of uncertainty and second-guessing prevails
◆ normally trustworthy mental functions like memory seem to fail
◆ if there is injury or death, the owner and employees can experience severe psychological stress and harm
◆ if a major time-waster occurs, feelings of failure and panic can set in

Once you begin to answer the "What-if?" and "Who can do it?" questions, then you are more likely to appreciate the time you put into applying an ounce of prevention to your structure and procedures rather than waiting for the dreaded pound of cure.

IDENTIFY A MEETING AREA

LARGE COMPANIES CALL THEM "WAR ROOMS," COMMAND centers, or crisis centers, and quite often these facilities sit empty just waiting to be used during a crisis. As a small business owner, you may not have enough space for day-to-day operations, let alone enough to dedicate to emergency response. And that's fine, but you should still designate a meeting place and equip the space with as many resources as you can so that you are free to concentrate on content, rather than setup, during adverse times.

A conference room is ideal as a meeting location because it will separate responders from their offices, which are filled with day-to-day distractions. When a crisis hits, it should be isolated and dealt with immediately. It helps to accomplish this if the responders are also isolated from distractions.

At a minimum, you will want to have the following available in your meeting area:

◆ diagrams of installations
◆ organization charts
◆ fact sheets on products and processes
◆ lists of key customers, suppliers, and any other contacts who should be informed of the situation
◆ telephone numbers and other contact information for all responders
◆ telephones
◆ computer terminals
◆ copy machine
◆ fax machines
◆ white boards or flip charts
◆ crisis plans, work sheets, or any materials that you prepared in advance to guide response

The size and nature of your business will factor into your decisions on how extensively to equip a crisis response location. Business owners who want a fully dedicated and equipped facility should think about what would be needed to deal with a serious emergency.

FACILITIES AND EQUIPMENT

IF YOU COULD CREATE THE PERFECT CRISIS-PLANNING SHOPping list, this would be it. You may be a small business and find it hard to store your day-to-day equipment, let alone think about equipping a space dedicated for use during unexpected situations. However, no doubt you hope to grow;

this list will help you secure what you can now and make you aware of what you'll need as you grow.

For now, identify the items you would not want to be without if you suddenly got caught by a crisis this afternoon. Then get to work securing them.

◆ **Facilities**

Command Center

Media Response Center

Others (perhaps a tent or makeshift dwelling you could set up if you experienced negative situations far from your office)

◆ **Facility considerations**

Primary location

Secondary (backup) location

Agreements with owners of these locations

Ample parking

Access to restrooms

Provisions for security

Electrical power (main supply)

Electrical power (backup supply)

Access to company computer network

Telephone, communications

Environmentally safe location, sustainable for long-term operations

Means of transportation to and from facilities

◆ **Special media response center considerations**

Company Work Area

— Private and secure

Media Briefing Area

— Accessible by news media

— Interview area

— Phones available for media (optional)

— Near crisis scene (if possible)

— Near hotels, restaurants (if possible)

◆ **Furniture**

Tables or desks

Chairs for emergency workers and media

Typewriter or computer stands

Storage lockers or cabinets

Portable file containers
Status boards
Flip charts and easels
White boards and markers
Wastebaskets
Podium, table, and chairs for press conferences
   (Media Response Center)

◆ **Equipment**
Photocopiers: Minimum of two
Fax machines: Minimum of one incoming and one outgoing
Computers and printers; cables and diskettes
Software for computers
Typewriters (as a backup)
Teleconferencing equipment
Telephones
Speakerphone(s)
Shredders
Coffeemaker
Clocks

◆ **Special media response center equipment**
Recording equipment
Video camera, monitors, VCRs, tapes
Audio tape recorders and cassettes
Sound equipment, microphones, cables, speakers
Audio distribution box
Television(s) and radio(s) for media monitoring

◆ **Supplies: All facilities**
Copies of crisis response plans
Company phone lists
Area and specialty phone books
Forms and logs to record events
Pens and pencils
Lined paper and pads
Fax paper (if needed) and fax cover sheets
Toner for photocopier and printer
Paper clips
Stapler and staples
Other office supplies
Access badges

Maps as applicable: site, community, county, region, sales, national

Plans: building layouts, floor layouts, site plans—all locations

Diagrams, charts as needed

Instant camera and film

Markers

Batteries

Tape (duct, masking, and clear)

Coffee, tea, cups, spoons, napkins, paper towels, etc.

Storage boxes

Extension cords

◆ **Additional media response center supplies**

Company stationery

Press release stationery

Visual aids

Company information, reports, etc.

Press kits

Typing paper

Dictionary and thesaurus

◆ **Considerations for mobile response**

Van or other vehicle

Tent or other portable structures

Footlockers, trunks, travel cases for storing and transporting supplies:

— Computer, printer (battery operated)

— Portable fax machine

— Cellular phone(s)

— Phone directories

— Stationery, paper, pens, markers

— Cash (bills and coins)

— Major credit card(s)

Telephone credit card

Personal travel kits (or list)

— Clothing

— Personal hygiene kits, supplies

— Glasses, contact lenses, cleaning supplies

— Aspirin and personal medications

Transportation

— Company vehicles

— Contracts with carriers, services: air, auto, boat

— Courier services

Provisions to access U.S. and international currency

Turn Adversity into Opportunity

MY NEWS PRODUCER FRIEND, JIM LEMAY, HAS COVERED MANY business crises in his time, and he says that a crisis is a company's defining moment. And he's right. A crisis is an unstable time in which a decisive change is impending. In other words, it's a turning point for better or worse—a time when the outcome could be very undesirable or extremely positive. I have seen many companies take advantage of a crisis, a turning point, and use it to increase awareness and understanding of what the business does.

The choice of the outcome can often be in the hands of the owner or manager handling the event. Of course, the exceptions to this might be those times when gross mismanagement is at fault. But if you run an honest and aboveboard business, then you may find that you have an opportunity when a crisis hits. Sure, it will still be a bother to deal with, but it can be an opportunity, too.

Why wouldn't any business owner make it a routine practice to plan for a turning point, to remove much of the risk and uncertainty to achieve more control over the outcome? Perhaps because many small businesses think that crisis plans are only for large corporations. Not so; every business, large or small, public or private, should review risks and establish plans. There are no exceptions to the need for a plan, only differences of degree based upon the size of the company and its potential risks. The best planning efforts simultaneously remove risks and add opportunity.

I'm often asked how a crisis can mean opportunity for a small business. The answer is to use the unexpected event to your advantage by making it a turning point to benefit your company. When that happens, then, ask yourself if you can use it to

◆ educate potential customers as to what your company is all about;

- strengthen your relationship with current customers;
- gain a lead on your competition;
- solidify your relationship with a supplier;
- win the support and allegiance of your employees;
- position yourself as a change agent within your industry;
- make changes faster than you could under normal circumstances; or
- emerge as a good guy with the public's interest in mind.

The bottom line is that any company that can plan for a turning point stands a better chance of taking advantage of that opportunity than one that is caught totally unprepared.

Conduct a Vulnerability Assessment of Your Company

TO DETERMINE IN WHAT AREAS YOUR COMPANY MAY BE VULNERable, conduct a vulnerability assessment.

Divide—with a pencil or word processor—a sheet of paper into three columns. At the top of the first column, write or type "Area of Concern." The second column should be labeled "Potential Problem," and the third, "Recommendations for Response."

Next, get together with employees at a predetermined time and give them guidance in completing the forms. It's important to tell employees—and to honor it!—that this form will remain confidential and that all concerns are legitimate.

You may need to offer some explanation for each column:

- **Column one.** This column should list an area of concern: problems, processes, complications, attitudes, opinions.
- **Column two.** Here, have employees state possible primary and secondary negative outcomes as a result of that problem. Encourage employees to think beyond one event at a time and instead to look at sequential events. For example, the accident at the Three Mile Island nuclear plant in 1979 was caused by several individual, smaller incidents. Everyone is capable of losing power; determine how long you can endure a power outage before you experience a substantial business loss.

◆ **Column three.** Employees should list here all actions needed to resolve or address both the area of concern (now) and the potential problems (during a crisis or unexpected event).

List only one concern per sheet. This will make it easier later to record thoughts and action items on each concern. Give the employees extra copies so that they continue to think about the concerns and can turn in other ideas later.

The second part of your employee brainstorming session will involve developing answers together to the following questions. You might find that these questions identify other vulnerabilities that were overlooked in step one above.

◆ What would we do if our facility were damaged enough to be closed for several days?

◆ What if it were totally destroyed?

◆ How would you quickly get in touch with one another to activate the backup plans?

◆ Could we operate somewhere else? Where? What could you do now to secure that location?

◆ How will you quickly transport items such as computers, inventory, and equipment?

◆ If you have backup supplies and equipment, are they stored in a place that is not vulnerable to the same disaster as your facility?

◆ What could we absolutely not survive without?

◆ What can we do to make sure we never have to live without them?

◆ What if there was a prolonged power outage? Do we have a backup generator to maintain services such as refrigeration, security, lighting, heat, and computer control?

◆ What if the local phone service were disabled for an indefinite time?

◆ What if a natural disaster struck and employees couldn't make it to work for several days?

◆ What if our key suppliers or shippers experienced a crisis even though we did not? Do we know or have relationships established with backup suppliers and shippers?

◆ What if our key customers no longer needed our product or services? Could we repackage, refocus, and market to anoth-

er audience? Who would that audience be? Could we diversify our product line more?

◆ What if our vital records were destroyed? Which paperwork
and records are necessary for the continuation and recovery
of our business?

◆ What if one of us were seriously injured or even killed here
at the facility? How should we deal with family members,
emergency crews, and the news media?

◆ Do we know how to find out which hospital an injured
employee has been taken to? Do we know how to obtain
updates on the injured person's status?

◆ Do we have a means set up to quickly inform customers and
suppliers of the company's ability or inability to fill orders
and supply services?

◆ Is our insurance adequate to get us back into operation? Do
we know without a doubt what we are covered for and what
we are not?

The third step in identifying potential problems is
preparing planning work sheets. Record the potential problems that were identified on the Vulnerability Identification Forms onto Planning Work Sheets, along with the
well-thought-through answers for each problem to the
subtopics below:

◆ Topic/concern

◆ Who needs to be notified (including external and internal
people)?

◆ Who within and outside the company can provide back-
ground/technical expertise or support?

◆ Overall objectives/desired outcome of response. (Describe
what the results would look like if they were handled perfectly.)

◆ Anticipated list of priorities. (What should the planning priorities be?)

◆ What is our primary strategy for achieving our desired outcome? (What actions should be taken now? By whom? What
can't be addressed until the unexpected occurs? How will
these actions be carried out? By whom? What support is
required?)

◆ What is our alternate strategy?

The Bottom Line

SO FAR YOU'VE BEEN INTRODUCED TO THE BASIC STEPS
involved in preparing for the unexpected so that when it happens, you can concentrate on the content of the crisis rather than on establishing an ad hoc emergency plan. However, there's more you can do to ease your vulnerability to a crisis, and that is to eliminate it—or as much of it as you can—in the first place. Chapter 2 will get your started. As you read that chapter, don't think about the hours it may take to do a thorough review of your business; instead, look upon that review as an investment in your company's future.

CHAPTER 2

Conduct a Small Business Self-Audit

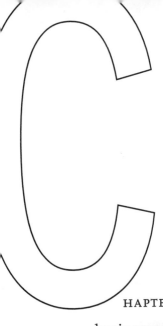

HAPTER 1 ASSUMES THAT YOU KNOW YOUR business well. But let's suppose you are like most other entrepreneurs: you have built a company around your expertise, or you excel in one or two areas and, therefore, may not recognize problems that might arise in other parts of the business. This chapter will help you do an exhaustive search for existing or potential problems that, if left unaddressed, might sneak up on you.

Big business calls these internal probes *audits* or *inspections,* and sets up elaborate committees and evaluation mechanisms to uncover weaknesses. As a small business, you don't have these luxuries, but you do have several things big businesses may not have: a strong familiarity with your employees and their understanding of your company, a basic gut instinct for where problems may surface, and your intuition to guide you in where and when to probe

more closely. Business journals are just beginning
to discover and to report on the use and value of
intuition in business.

Preventing Problems

SO FAR YOU'VE READ CHAPTER 1 AND GOTTEN A SENSE
of where your company may be vulnerable to mis-
haps and crises. You've also begun plotting how
you'll set up a team, where they'll meet, and how
they'll organize to tackle the unexpected when it
hits. Through the vulnerability assessment, you may
even have begun listing areas in which you can
make corrective actions now. The Small Business
Self-Audit below will help you identify risks that you
can eliminate. After all, being able to weather and
conquer a crisis is a good thing, but all the cleanup
in the world is not as good as preventing problems
in the first place. This chapter is designed to help

you uncover potential problems and smoldering situations. Following each set of questions, you will find explanations, along with guidance for identifying and eliminating the risks. For obvious serious threats (such as theft and fire), more in-depth information and suggestions have been provided. For others, you will find more guidance throughout the remainder of this book.

A Comprehensive Search for Potential Problems

IN THIS SELF-AUDIT, MOST CATEGORIES OF GOOD BUSINESS management are addressed, from general bookkeeping and accounting practices to financial planning to personnel, with more in between. However, the focus of this book and this audit is to prepare you for the unexpected, not to dictate good management practices, although often the two go hand in hand. For example, good management would dictate that you attend trade shows to make contacts and stay abreast of state-of-the-art technology. However, you won't find this item on the list because there is no direct correlation between not attending a trade show and experiencing problems; unless, of course, your company does all its business at trade shows. Likewise, thousands of marketing, advertising, and promotional techniques could be employed that would make your business grow and thrive, but *not* carrying out any of these ideas will not necessarily result in a crisis.

As you go through the audit, think in terms of *safeguarding* your company rather than *growing* your company. You should conduct a separate audit with a more applicable list of items for the latter. This audit is all about safeguarding and identifying potential problems. For example, consider the question, "Does the company have an annual budget?" For the purposes of this book, the question is not posed to ensure that you can track your cash flow, which is essential to good management; instead, the question is included to get you thinking about the flow of your money into, through, and out of the business. If you find something amiss with your budget, it could suggest embezzlement, wasteful spending, or any of a series of situations that could create a budgetary crisis.

Be sure to answer all questions. At times you may wonder why a question is included when alone it could not lead directly to a crisis. For example, it's rather obvious how an unattended fire in a garbage can might lead directly to a crisis; however, it may not be as obvious how an unequitable distribution of work could lead to trouble. In the latter situation, the route to problems might be a bit indirect: unfair work practices can lead to frustration or anger that can lead to a variety of negative consequences, from low morale to workplace violence. Low morale creates a negative atmosphere that customers can pick up on. Eventually customers stop frequenting places that are not friendly and customer-oriented. In the end, with no customers, you have no business.

And finally, as you answer each question, think through the ripple effect each item could have on other aspects of your business. For example, if you experience a situation that results in lost revenue, you may also face contractual fines or penalties if you cannot meet your obligations. Or if you experience a flood, your problems may go beyond equipping your office with dry computers and diskettes from your backup location: the negative publicity about the flooded area may affect your ability to attract customers back to your place of business.

As you conduct the self-audit, keep good notes and mark each "no" answer. These are the areas you will want to address first.

The Self-Audit

MISSION STATEMENT

◆ Do we have a clear mission statement?
◆ Are we carrying out the mission?
◆ Do employees understand and support the mission?

A mission statement doesn't have to be elaborate, but it must be clearly defined. It must state conclusively what business you are in, who your target market is, and what you do to serve that market. If you can't define clearly what your business is all about, your customers may never understand what you can do for them, so they'll go elsewhere; your employees may not understand their role in carrying out the mission, so they'll create another self-serving mission instead; and your bankers and investors certainly won't be inclined to give you additional funds, and that can be disastrous when you need help the most.

BUSINESS PLAN

◆ Do we have a written business plan?
◆ Is that business plan thorough enough to share with loan officers when seeking a loan?

Your business plan explains the route you're going to take in order to fulfill your mission. It's a necessary document that loan officers will demand to see before they lend you the necessary funds in a pinch. And most importantly—in keeping with the focus of this book—a business plan is a valuable reference document if you experience a crisis; when you're faced with response options, the plan will serve as a reminder of what you will want to have accomplished when the crisis is over.

BUDGET

◆ Do we have and follow an annual budget?
◆ Is the budget realistic?
◆ Is the budget used as a control device?
◆ Are actual expenditures compared against budgeted expenditures, and corrections made for the future?

You need to establish and stick to a budget if you want to monitor and control expenses. Financial troubles usually start when companies don't take corrective actions when expenses are over budget. Also, be cautious in granting permission to employees to spend beyond budget. In general, as owner or manager of the business, you should be the one who sets the budget and the financial controls. Handing over control of the budget is, in effect, handing over control of the business. If you delegate these responsibilities to a financial officer, then build in a system of checks and balances that requires you to periodically review the budget. After all, if it's company policy, then the financial officer won't be insulted when you want to take a closer look, and that person will think twice about doing creative bookkeeping.

FINANCES

- ◆ Do we have a good bookkeeping system?
- ◆ Are our books and records up-to-date?
- ◆ If the bookkeeping is outsourced, do we hold regular meetings with the bookkeeper/accountant?
- ◆ Do we reconcile bank statements monthly?
- ◆ Are all obligations paid promptly?
- ◆ Do we prepare and review financial statements?
- ◆ Are the statements compared against industry averages?
- ◆ Are a balance sheet and income statements readily available to show lenders?
- ◆ Do appropriate officers of the company know the financial status of the business at all times?
- ◆ Is customer invoicing done promptly?
- ◆ Are customers paying promptly?
- ◆ Do we have a credit policy?
- ◆ Is the policy flexible enough to accommodate unusual customer situations but rigid enough to be respected?
- ◆ Are payrolls met without a problem?
- ◆ Do we make regular deposits for federal withholding and Social Security taxes?
- ◆ Do we file all tax returns on time?
- ◆ Is money set aside for expansion and unexpected situations?
- ◆ Do we have a good working relationship with a banker?
- ◆ Could we pay creditors and employees during a prolonged shutdown?

The importance of a solid financial foundation is best explained in the results of a study conducted for the U.S. Small Business Administration, "Financial Difficulties of Small Businesses and Reasons for Their Failure." Financial problems were cited 28 percent of the time as reasons why small businesses declare bankruptcy. These financial problems include high debt, loss of financing, and the inability to get financing. Taxes were credited with being the cause of bankruptcy more than 20 percent of the time.

You will want to have a good relationship with your bankers and have your paperwork ready at all times. Loans may be necessary in a pinch, and if the paperwork and the approval process are not done in advance, you will lose precious time. A lender will want to see your business plan, the company balance sheet (the major yardstick for solvency), and the income statement (the common measure for profits).

You can learn more about dealing with lenders and strengthening your cash flow in Chapter 3, "Avoid the Most Common Management Missteps."

SALES

◆ Do we have a written sales plan?
◆ Do sales figures support that the plan is sound?
◆ Has our target market been appropriately identified?
◆ Has the target market been reached?
◆ Are customers polled to determine their satisfaction?
◆ Are new products and services developed regularly or, at a minimum, when needed?
◆ Are prices set competitively?

Good sales planning is instrumental to a positive cash flow. It begins with knowing who your target audience is and how you can reach them. If you're reaching the wrong audience, you might run out of money quickly. If sales aren't increasing, it could be a sign of a smoldering crisis: your pricing structure is off, market demand has changed, your product or service is poorly developed or delivered, or advertising isn't appropriate. If you find your sales are going down and you are losing customers, then read Chapter 3, "Avoid the Most Common Management Missteps."

PRICING

◆ Can we justify the prices we charge?
◆ Do we provide volume discounts?
◆ Are prices increased when necessary?

You should determine an effective pricing policy, based on your mission, your budget, and your target market, instead of merely setting your prices a fraction less than your competition's. Your prices should be tailored to your own unique situation and what you need to charge to turn a profit. However, if your prices differ dramatically from those of similar items in the market, then you had better offer other features to justify the difference. Remember basic marketing principles: your goal isn't to build a better mousetrap but rather to build a different mousetrap. Then your task becomes making sure your prospects are aware of the added features that make you different. It's important too that you raise prices when your expenses go up; otherwise, you may be setting yourself up for financial problems down the road.

PERSONNEL

◆ Do employees know what is expected of them?
◆ Are they adequately trained to carry out their jobs?
◆ Does each employee report directly to just one person?
◆ Do all employees have job descriptions they can understand?
◆ Is the workload distributed equitably and fairly?
◆ Are employees familiar with company policies?
◆ Do employees get feedback on their performance?
◆ Are employees immediately informed when performance is below expectation?
◆ Is there a solid hiring procedure?
◆ Is there a solid firing procedure?
◆ Are systems in place to prevent employee theft?
◆ Do employees feel comfortable volunteering negative information to management?
◆ Are OSHA standards followed to protect employees?
◆ Is there a written sexual harassment policy?
◆ Are policies for vacations, sick leave, absences, hiring, and firing written down and available for anyone to review at any time?

Much has been written about the benefits of good employee relations, yet every day, companies experience problems that can be linked to apathy, ignorance, dishonesty, or poor training. The questions in this category are designed to get you thinking about your responsibility to your employees and their responsibility to the company. The Institute for Crisis Management reports that employees cause roughly 14 percent of business crises (see Chapter 3). The bottom line in a crisis is even though an employee may cause a situation, it's still your problem to deal with. When the event is reported in the news, reporters will generally use your company name, not that of the employee. If OSHA standards or discrimination guidelines have not been met, ignorance of the law is no excuse.

SUPPLIERS

◆ Are two or more suppliers identified and available for each product needed?

◆ Are other sources identified that can provide raw materials in an emergency?

◆ Does the supplier have contingency plans they have shared with us?

◆ Are delivery times established and adhered to?

◆ Are payment terms clearly documented?

◆ Do we conduct regular incoming inventory inspections?

When one of your suppliers is hit with a crisis and cannot deliver goods or services, your business may experience a loss, too. Many businesses depend on daily deliveries, such as desserts to a restaurant or parts to a repair shop. You will want to have written contracts with your suppliers since they are so critical to your survival. These agreements should include delivery schedules, payment terms, standards of quality for your purchases, and backup plans in case they can't deliver or you can't receive the merchandise. However, even though a contract may be in your favor if you go to court, it's still not going to get you the materials you need if your supplier is shut down: you should make an occasional purchase from a supplier outside of your local area, so you will have an alternate source from which to obtain critical items.

CUSTOMER RELATIONS

◆ Do employees treat customers courteously?

◆ Are customers' complaints addressed immediately, adequately, and courteously?

◆ Do customers reward us with repeat sales? Do they recommend us to others?

◆ Does the company solicit feedback?

- Does the company keep a database of customers for future communication and demographic research?
- Are sales goals being met?
- Have we guarded against loss of customer base by diversifying product lines, sales locations, or target customers?
- Do we have alternative plans in case our key customers no longer need our product or services? If so, could we repackage, refocus, and market to another audience? Do we know who that audience would be?

Given the 80/20 rule—that 80 percent of your business will come from 20 percent of your customers—then it only makes sense that you strive to keep customers happy and stay in touch with their needs. For more ideas on enhancing the employee-customer relationship, see Chapter 4, "Practice the Personnel Touch with Employees."

LOCATION

- Is our location appropriate for the business and the work we do?
- Is the location relatively free of threats of natural disasters (floods, earthquakes, freezing temperatures)?
- Is the location easily accessible?
- Is the environment around the office free of potential hazards?
- Is the office clean, neat, safe, and brightly lit?
- Is the office equipped with fire protection equipment and warning devices?
- Is a first aid kit available? Do employees know where it is and how to use it?
- Do we have a guaranteed backup location where we could meet if our office was closed for several days or totally destroyed?

All businesses should post evacuation maps that show the fastest and safest ways out of the building and list emergency numbers such as police, fire, and ambulance. Pick an anniversary date—for example, the day clocks are changed twice a year—to verify that all phone numbers are up-to-date. This would also be an opportune time to check fire alarms and extinguishers and stage a fire drill.

A good reason to keep backup files and documents in a separate location is the possibility of your becoming eligible for tax breaks to offset losses following a crisis. In many cases it's possible to take a deduction for the actual property loss from damage to your business property. But what this means is that you will need good documentation, not only of the destruction but of the property before it was damaged, through records, receipts, and descriptions. For this reason, your first and easiest safeguards against such disasters are to keep your records in order, back them up, and store copies at two separate locations.

Floods are the chief natural disaster to strike small businesses. You should consider flooding as a potential threat if you are located on a floodplain, near a river, downstream from a dam, or in an area with a high water table. Also, if you are located in a potential earthquake region, be aware that earthquakes can reroute rivers, empty lakes, destroy dams, and bring down the local water tower. Floods also occur in areas that are not designed to handle a deep freeze. Water mains can break and pipes can burst. The result is generally flooding when the water thaws.

Know what your insurance does not cover. Most general casualty policies do not cover flood damage. Don't assume that just because it never happened before, it never will. Flooding patterns are changed by both industrial and domestic development. Water that runs off new streets and parking lots may overwhelm nearby streams, surrounding lands, and parking lots. There may be a good reason that you got the building or office space at such a reasonable price: the stream beside your building may now be a gentle flow of water that has never flooded, but a downpour could turn it into a destructive torrent that erodes your building foundation. Plan for the worst.

In any disaster, people may be trapped and unable to leave even if they want to. This means that if you have more than a home-based business you should consider throwing some extra supplies in a supply cabinet located on the second floor or higher, such as:

◆ **Clean potable water.** The federal government recommends at least one gallon per person per day.

- **Towels, blankets, and warm clothing.** Keeping dry is an important prevention against exposure. People can get sick and/or die quickly if they lose core body heat.
- **Heating devices.** You may have to dry yourself, your clothing, and your blankets, and you may have to cook food. You will need a stove with independent fuel. Electricity and gas may not be available.
- **Human waste disposal containers.** Disposal may not be possible for a while, so human waste may need to be stored.
- **Ropes.** Keep them on hand to serve as lifelines or for escape from windows.

ENVIRONMENTAL IMPACT

- Are we complying with all regulations to keep the environment clean?
- Do we dispose of wastes properly?
- Do we store, ship, and dispose of hazardous wastes appropriately?
- Are we clear about what constitutes a hazardous waste?

As with OSHA rules, ignorance of the law is no excuse. If you damage the environment, you may be held liable whether or not you understand your responsibilities. According to statistics from the Environmental Protection Agency (EPA), more than 150 million Americans live in areas where air pollution levels violate federal health standards. Further, more than 350 billion pounds of chemicals are produced each year in the United States, or more than 1,000 pounds for every person. The majority of this pollution and these chemicals comes from businesses. If you don't have a thorough understanding of the environmental regulations that govern your business, you run the risk of government-imposed fines. If you are uncertain which regulations apply to your business, the EPA can provide the answers through its EPA Asbestos and Small Business Ombudsman Hotline, 800-368-5888. The purpose of this office is to help small companies comply with all types of federal environmental regulation.

If you are confused by regulations for hazardous waste, then talk to the experts at the EPA at their hazardous waste hotline: 800-424-9346. Rusty canisters leaking green sludge are not the poster picture for hazardous materials anymore; instead, our modern perils consist of printing fluids, dry-cleaning wastes, and some used oils. Even some rinse water can qualify as hazardous to human health. Further, the following items may qualify as hazardous wastes too, depending upon the type and concentration: pesticides, petroleum products, dyes, paints, thinners, solvents, cleaning fluids, flammable materials, and materials that dissolve metals, wood, or clothing.

EQUIPMENT AND VEHICLES

◆ Are employees appropriately trained in how to operate company equipment and vehicles?

◆ Is that training documented?

◆ Are vital equipment and vehicles on a schedule for regular maintenance?

◆ Is the schedule established such that no two vital machines or vehicles will be undergoing maintenance work at the same time?

◆ Is the log available for repair personnel to review?

◆ Do we have written arrangements with computer vendors to quickly replace damaged vital hardware?

Imagine explaining to the news media why you don't have a service record for the company vehicle that was just involved in a fatal accident. As for equipment: keep invoices, shipping lists, and other documentation of your system configuration off-site so you can quickly order the correct replacement components if necessary. Take care of credit checks, purchase accounts, and other vendor requirements in advance so that the vendor can ship replacements immediately.

LEGAL MATTERS

◆ Do we have access to legal advice twenty-four hours a day?

◆ Are contracts and leases honored by all parties named in the contract?

◆ Is legal counsel sought anytime suggestions or hints of misconduct are identified?

◆ Are company personnel policies reviewed by an attorney before being implemented?

- Are employee problems routinely documented?
- Is training made available by an outside third party when employees break with company policy, such as in a harassment issue? Is such training also part of the normal orientation for all employees, so we're not just waiting until there's a problem?
- Have we addressed all areas that look to the outside world like developing crises?

In the SBA report reasons for business failures mentioned earlier, nearly one in five owners listed legal disputes with customers, banks, mortgage companies, landlords, suppliers, franchisers, employees, or neighbors. For more than half of the businesses, the dispute had already escalated to a formal legal action.

It is an especially good idea to correct those situations in which it's obvious to others that your business is vulnerable. After all, most attorneys (and juries) interpret the law thus: you may not be *required* to have an emergency plan depending upon the line of work you are in, but you can be held liable if something happens and you *don't* have one. Based upon this catch-22, it's a good idea to develop plans for those times when you may be especially susceptible and the safety of employees and neighbors may be in jeopardy.

COMMUNICATION

- Have we identified the people we need to contact during an emergency?
- Do we have reliable channels set up to communicate with these key contacts?
- Will we still be able to use those channels during a crisis?
- Do we have backup plans for reaching contacts?

Many problems—especially smoldering crises—start with poor communication. When it comes to planning, it's important to remember that no company is an island. The same people that you rely on day to day to support your company may become even more important during a crisis. Others—those who are not essential in a crisis situation— will assume that because they are important on a daily basis, they should get individual attention and immediate

Key Contacts

- Employees
- Employees' families
- Sales agents
- Legal counsel
- Financial counsel
- Lending officers
- Public relations counsel
- Security officers
- Shareholders/investors
- Suppliers and vendors
- Distributors
- General contractors
- Unions
- Clients/customers
- News media
- Company neighbors and local residents
- General public
- Community leaders
- Local government agency representatives
- Politicians
- Local police
- Local fire departments
- Ambulance services
- Hospitals
- Competition
- Clergy

answers to their questions *during* a crisis. Still others may not be essential on a daily basis but may have information that you need. Finally, you may be forced to give attention to unexpected audiences, such as competitors who try to take advantage of your situation. For each key contact listed above, determine the following:

- Do you know how you will reach them during a crisis?
- Do you have contact information available in two separate locations?
- Do you know what they will expect from you?
- Do you know how they can help or hurt you?

CURRENT CONTINGENCY PLANS

- Do we know what to do if our facility is damaged enough to be closed for several days?
- Do we know what to do if it is totally destroyed?
- Do we know what to do if a natural disaster strikes and employees can't make it to work for several days?
- Do employees know how to get in touch with one another to activate the backup plans?
- Could we operate somewhere else?

- Do we know where that would be, and have we done everything we can now to secure that location?
- Do we have a means set up to inform customers and suppliers quickly of the company's ability or inability to fill orders and supply services?
- Have we identified files, equipment, tools, custom-made parts, etc., we would need to continue operations elsewhere?
- Have we worked out how to transport these items quickly?
- Are duplicate backup items stored in a place that is not vulnerable to the same disaster as our facility?
- Do we have a backup generator to maintain full services, such as refrigeration, security, lighting, heat, and computer control, in case of a prolonged power outage?
- Do we have backup plans in case the local phone service is disabled?
- Do employees know what to do if there is a telephone outage?
- Do we know what to do if one of us were seriously injured or even killed here at the company offices? (Do we know how to deal with family members, emergency crews, the news media?)

- Have we met in person with our local government emergency services office and fire department to know how they will respond in an emergency at our offices?
- Have we installed permanent shutters (to combat wind-borne debris) or safety gates (to curtail crime) over windows and doors?

THREAT OF FIRE

FIRE IS LISTED AS ITS OWN CONSIDERATION ON THIS AUDIT because statistically, small businesses suffer from fires more than any other nonadministrative or nonpersonnel emergency. Here are some questions to consider:

- Do we have an adequate and functioning fire suppression system?
- Are our employees trained on what to do in case of fire?
- Have we acquainted the local fire department with any unique or challenging features of our facility and products?

While it's true that most businesses carry insurance to

safeguard against loss due to fire, insurance generally cannot make up for *all* your lost time, revenue, and customer fulfillment until you recover from the fire. By the time you've opened your doors again, you may find that your customers have taken their business elsewhere.

The best fire-elimination technique is to prevent the fire in the first place. Make your employees aware of where flammables are kept. Don't allow smoking in the building. Be aware of the potential of a fire in a neighboring building.

My friend Mike, an accountant, has an office beside a potpourri shop that continually burns scented candles so that customers can savor the sweet smell the moment they walk in the door. Of course, I think it's a great idea for the shop owner to carry loads of fire insurance. And she does. But I also advised Mike to carry extra fire insurance too, since by mere location he is more susceptible to a fire emergency than other accountants might be.

The law dictates how many approved fire extinguishers a business must have based upon its line of work, its size, and many other factors. Be sure you comply with the requirements for your business, and then, to be on the safe side, exceed those requirements.

It doesn't take just electrical problems, oily rags, heating elements, and gas leaks to cause fires. Earthquakes, tornadoes, and high winds can often result in fires. And fires can be set intentionally. The best prevention for fires due to arson is to beef up your security measures.

Hold practice fire drills. Drills protect more than people and facilities—they also can protect you from legal hassles. So conduct drills, get signatures from participants, and document the events. Be sure to keep a backup record in a different location.

When practicing a fire drill, make sure everyone knows how to dial 911 or other emergency numbers from every phone. Some phones carry so many buttons that they can be confusing for some employees to use. When a phone is out of order, label it so that time is not lost in trying to get a dial tone.

Establish a word or phrase, such as "Scram" or "Out" or "Clear the office", that will indicate to everyone that they are to leave immediately, not even stopping for coats. And make sure that each exit has been clearly marked, that they are lighted at night, and that paths are clear.

Along with designating a meeting place and taking roll, have at least one person assigned the task of informing neighbors immediately that there is a fire at your location.

And finally, install alarms in the building. If your building houses several businesses, the alarm system should extend throughout.

When Ann King watched her building burn to the ground in 1993, her company, Atlanta-based Blooming Cookies Catalog Co., was relatively small and young. She and her partner had total insurance coverage of only $25,000, and the fire ended up costing over $300,000 in equipment and inventory loss alone. Ann's best advice: "Keep your insurance updated with replacement cost. We had grown anywhere from 20 percent to 35 percent annually, but our insurance did not reflect those numbers. Unfortunately, we were trying to cut corners."

Other advice from Ann:

- ◆ **Add security.** "Insist that the building be kept under surveillance camera and that law enforcement cruise the surrounding area."

- ◆ **Add a fire suppression system.** "Our building was old and the owners were not willing to spend the money. But I wish we had."

- ◆ **Have your records in order, copied, and filed at a second location.** "We were the prime suspects in the beginning until the inspectors came in and reviewed our paperwork and our finances. We were made to feel guilty, or at least suspect, until proven innocent. The owners of the building's insurance company started haggling with our insurance company over who would pay for what. Of course, had we been proven to have started the fire, we would have been responsible for everything and their insurance would not be liable for rebuilding."

- ◆ **Have a backup location designated and ready.** "All of the paperwork involved was a nightmare, as was all of the time it took setting up a new relationship with a new bakery, setting up phone systems, cleaning the smoke damage, and waiting another three months for the building to be rebuilt, all the while trying to gear up to head into our Christmas season."

◆ **Don't assume false safety.** Just because you have no enemies or disgruntled employees doesn't mean that you won't be the victim of arson. The fire that destroyed the Blooming Cookies facility was set by an arsonist who was a stranger to Ann and her staff. As she later learned, "He had walked by our building frequently and had become intrigued by our mural painted on the outside wall. The mural looked like a garden with trees and cookie flowers growing. He originally said he broke in just to rob us, but after walking around for a few hours and eating cookies, he decided [the place] would make a great fire. So he set it on fire and then walked outside and sat on a hill and watched it burn. Meanwhile, sixty-five-foot flames were leaping from the building as twelve fire trucks worked to put it out."

◆ **Walk through the scenario of losing everything to a fire.** Plan now what you would do if you were to lose all your assets to a fire. "At first we were completely numb, but I think we whipped into action rather quickly. We knew we had to; we couldn't stop and feel sorry for ourselves, and we could not give up like so many of our friends and family encouraged us to do. To say that we felt vulnerable would be an understatement. Initially we were scared that the arsonist might come back and finish the business off. We were not sure if it was an angry ex-employee who knew where our homes were and might target those as well. Then, because the building could not be secured at night, someone broke in the first night after the fire and stole the music equipment and some inventory from production. Even the insurance adjuster's camera was stolen while he was there investigating the following day."

◆ **Seek advice from your insurance carrier or the fire department.** Both will generally provide a walk-through of your facility at no charge. They may be able to spot potential fire hazards that your untrained eye cannot. Be sure to document the walk-through by recording dates, time, people involved, areas assessed, and results. King would be the first to tell you that the effort is worth the time.

Fortunately, Blooming Cookies has grown to $3.5 million in sales, growing at a rate of 30 to 35 percent a year and selling to 60,000 customers around the world.

THEFT

◆ Do we have mechanisms established to discourage theft?
◆ Do employees know the punishment for stealing?
◆ Are employees alert to early warning signals of potential theft, such as groups of juveniles or customers carrying concealment devices?
◆ Do we keep small items of high value near or behind the counter?
◆ Do we use security devices (electronic sensing devices, two-way mirrors, cameras, etc.) to discourage theft?

According to SBA estimates, dishonest employees account for about two-thirds of retail theft, and shoplifting for the remaining one-third. Further, few outside burglars are ever caught: almost 80 percent of burglaries go unsolved. You cannot eliminate theft completely, but you can take steps to minimize it. Here are several steps to take:

◆ Screen job applicants thoroughly through personal interviews, reference checks, credit checks, and psychological tests.
◆ Expect excellence from your employees, and live up to that standard yourself.
◆ Set fair and reasonable rules and enforce them.
◆ Make sure employee reporting chains are clear.
◆ Establish a climate of accountability.
◆ Remove opportunities and temptations to steal. (For example: Give keys only to employees who need to have them. Keep supplies neat, organized, and inventoried. Discourage employees from working late solo. Open the mail yourself.)
◆ Secure the building or office (locks, guards if necessary, security systems, pull-down bars).
◆ Establish audit control methods with the books.
◆ Prosecute employees caught stealing. (Slapping their wrists or accepting an apology tells other employees what they can get away with, too.)

◆ Permit only authorized employees to set prices and mark merchandise (using rubber stamps or machines, not handwriting).

◆ Watch out for over-ring slips that cover up shortages.

◆ Install closed-circuit television, if possible, in pertinent areas, such as the stock room and the loading dock.

◆ Keep a close eye on juveniles in your shop. The SBA reports that young people account for almost 50 percent of all shoplifting.

◆ Train employees to be on the lookout for customers who act nervous and who carry concealing containers.

SABOTAGE AND TAINTED PRODUCTS

◆ Do we practice quality controls?

◆ Do employees abide by standards of excellence?

◆ Are outsiders kept away from vital areas where products are created or manufactured?

◆ Are security controls set up in storage areas?

◆ Do we take seriously any complaints or rumors of ill will from the outside?

◆ Do we conduct periodic inspections of the quarters where products are made and packaged?

A company doesn't have to be the size of Intel or Johnson and Johnson to experience a scare from sabotage or a tainted product. Our society is litigious, and consumers sometimes go after corporations to capitalize on the negative aftereffects of having consumed or experienced bad results from a tainted product. Although large companies are usually targeted due to their potential for heftier payoffs, this doesn't mean that small companies need not worry.

The moment your product leaves your premises, it is vulnerable to tampering, accidental or intended. And sometimes a product can be jeopardized on your premises, as was the case in 1996 for the small California Annabelle Candy Company.

In this case, says Annabelle's co-owner, president and CEO Susan Gamson Karl, a consumer bit into an Annabelle's rocky-road candy bar and encountered a meal moth. "It was the same kind of little bug you get in your flour at home. After hiring a new pest control company, suing the former one, and doing extensive assessments, we determined that the bug could have gotten into the candy bar in one of two ways: (1) we opened a door to throw out the trash and one flew in, or (2) it was in the peanuts we received."

Although the moth was determined by health, food, and safety experts to have posed no health dangers, Karl says that "it was still disgusting, and our rocky-road bar has never actually recovered. Our distribution and sales flattened and stayed flat."

Karl says that quality control is of utmost importance. "Pest control is a concern among all candy makers, and it was for us, too. At the time the moth was found, we were exterminating dutifully once each week. But I learned that it's not enough to be taking precautionary measures. You need to make sure that your controls are effective." Karl also says that since the incident, Annabelle's has developed crisis response plans, with a clearly designated team that would come together to handle the situation while other team members would continue day-to-day operation. For more on the lessons Annabelle's learned, see Chapter 7, "Brace Yourself for Negative Publicity and Public Scrutiny."

Your Next Step

IF YOU'VE DONE A THOROUGH REVIEW OF THE SELF-AUDIT, then you will probably have a list of items that you want to address and correct in your business. But wait! Your research isn't finished yet. The rest of this book is designed to give you more guidance as you tackle the task of preparing your company for the unexpected.

Getting
Your
House
in Order

SECT

CHAPTER 3

Avoid the Most Common Management Missteps

OMETIMES THE LEAST EXPECTED—YET most damaging—crisis to emerge from Pandora's box is one that could have been avoided simply by changing the way we do business. One of my favorite scenes from the children's movie *Snow White and the Seven Dwarfs* is the one in which the dwarfs end their working day by locking the door to the diamond mine and then hanging the key beside the lock. As small-business managers, the dwarfs follow the accepted principles of good management (put a lock on your door) but fail to think through all the what-ifs regarding what to do with the key.

That "what to do with the key" incorporates the way you do business. I have seen many small businesses come and go in nearly twelve years of business ownership and consulting. Many had a good chance of survival but failed because of poor policies, supervision, administration, or planning;

in other words, the aspects that define the management of the organization.

Then, to add gasoline to the fire when the adverse situation is identified, the business owner or manager refuses to recognize the situation as critical, or refuses to learn from the incident, which allows the mistakes to grow. The person who heads a business must: (a) identify and capitalize on the company's strengths, and (b) identify and learn from the company's mistakes. The most important lesson of all is never to repeat the same mistake.

This chapter will give you a heads-up on the most frequent crises and critical situations related to mismanagement that other small-business owners have experienced, from poor cash flow to losing customers to gearing up for a recession. In each case the entries have been brought together in this chapter because the crisis stemmed from the company's management—its administration and policies. With this knowledge, you will be able to troubleshoot potentially negative situations by removing as much risk as you can.

To successfully overcome each of the situations discussed in this chapter, as well as other negative circumstances, you may have to do the following:

◆ **Be receptive to outsiders' opinions and impressions of your company.** Often the person who will be able to offer you the best insight into your company's image or status in the community is an objective outsider: another business owner, a friend or neighbor you can trust to tell the truth, or a customer. Provide the latter with "Tell us what you think" or "How can we serve you better?" cards that they can fill out and turn in anonymously. Then give serious consideration to what they say.

◆ **Be receptive when insiders voice concern.** Your vulnerability to a smoldering situation is going to be even worse if you have established a culture—real or imagined—that "kills the messenger." If employees fear that dismissal, reprimand, or anger will follow the delivery of bad news, they'll keep it to themselves. Several years ago, employees in the radiology department of a hospital in Muncie, Indiana, believed some patients were being overdosed with radioactive isotopes. However, they said nothing, fearing reprisal by their supervisor. Eventually, an ex-employee leaked the situation to the press and the story appeared, causing damage to the hospital's reputation and finances.

◆ **Analyze these negative opinions objectively.** Business owners and top management will often deny a problem's existence or minimize the seriousness of its potential damage to the business. One famous such case was that of the England-based Barings Bank, whose management failed to deal with the financial discrepancies of one of its most successful traders in 1995. After the bank was destroyed by his actions, employee Nick Leeson was accused of forging documents and deceiving Barings and the Singapore International Monetary Exchange in an effort to make them believe that he had enough money to cover his losses. Some reports claimed that Leeson's bosses had not adequately controlled his trades and were aware of some of the crooked bookkeeping he did to hide the mounting losses. In that case, denial caused billions of dollars in losses and ultimately forced the bank to fail.

◆ **Find a safe ground or balance between the overly optimistic belief that company ingenuity can save the day and research and industry trends that indicate otherwise.** Fortunately, it's easy to get information on the state of the economy and the trends in your industry. Business reports fill the pages of magazines, and cable brings us a variety of business news shows. If you hear indications of downturns in your line of business, then take them seriously. Be willing to make changes.

◆ **Admit when your company needs to make changes or needs help.** Don't wait until it's too late. When the home improvement superstores and the megabookstores began popping up throughout America, it was just a matter of time before they moved into small towns and put mom-and-pop hardware stores and independent booksellers out of business. Many of these small stores still survive, however, thanks mostly to the owners' creativity and their willingness to make changes—to diversify, specialize, refocus their marketing, or beef up customer service.

◆ **Determine the nature of the problem and the type of change or help that is needed.** Seek the right counsel. There are many professionals, consultants, and small-business organizations who can assist you (see resources). If an employee has identified a potential problem, ask him how he thinks the situation could be resolved. When customers complain, go out of your way to meet with them to find out what led to their displeasure—even if they claim they will never do business with you again.

◆ **Take prompt action to solve the problem once you have determined what needs to be done.** Why wait? If a problem has been identified and you recognize that a change should be made, then do it as soon as possible. Remember from Chapter 1, smoldering crises afflict companies more often than sudden crises, and they can do more harm to the company's stability.

Let's look at an example of promptly solving a problem.

Let's say that you run a business with a staff of ten people. Being the overly cautious type, you still handle the payroll yourself. It's the day before payday, but customers are late in making payments, so you're short on cash. Because you anticipated this event, even planned for it, you call your banker and immediately set up a short-term loan. You're happy. Your employees are none the wiser. The customers don't know your situation, and the banker thinks you're an intelligent businessperson.

Now let's walk through that payroll scenario in a different way. This time, when you find yourself short on cash, you call the banker but are not granted a loan because you didn't establish the credit line in advance. You are forced to tell employees that they will not be paid on time. They become nervous to learn that you can't even meet your payroll. Their families become disgruntled and talk to neighbors and friends, and before long rumor establishes your company as a temporary resident in your town.

Now let's take a third shot at the same scenario. You have the same cash flow problem but have a line of credit established. Unfortunately, you are out of town and have delegated payroll to your assistant. The assistant, not aware of the cash situation, writes the checks (which you signed in advance) and pays employees. The checks bounce, thus putting your credibility with the banker in jeopardy. The bank calls your office to inform you that because you have a line of credit, they will cover the checks. But unfortunately, this alerts your employees to your unstable cash situation. They talk to family members, and the same scenario in our second example is played out.

But that's not all. In the second and third scenarios, enough talk flies through the town that your suppliers hear about the situation and begin to get nervous. They refuse to extend more credit and demand payment on your outstanding balance. Since you're not able to meet their demand, you, in turn, cannot meet customer demand. Customers begin to look elsewhere, and you watch your competitors grow. Meanwhile, because employees are nervous, they look for other jobs. Some go to the competition, taking with them complete knowledge of your company. Before long, you are forced to take drastic action.

As you prepare advertisements for your going-out-of-business sale or complete paperwork for Chapter 11 protection, you chastise yourself for: (a) not having established a line of credit in advance, when you knew, just knew, you carried a potential risk of unavailable cash, or (b) not telling your employees about the loan when you knew, just knew, that an informed employee makes a better employee. This chapter, like all the other chapters in this book, is all about removing risk and uncertainty from as many situations as possible and putting you in control of your destiny.

Signs of Impending Common Crises

YOU BEGIN TO QUESTION YOUR MANAGEMENT SKILLS

TOTAL QUALITY MANAGEMENT. STRATEGIC MANAGEMENT. Product management. Financial management. Hands-off management. Management by exception. Management by objectives. Management by walking around. What does it all mean? And which is best for your company? Is it possible to combine and practice them all?

You could earn an M.B.A. from Harvard and still not have perfect answers to these questions. Certainly there are enough books and classes available to introduce business owners to all the varying styles of management. Yet on a regular basis, business news coverage tells us about another company that failed due to "poor management."

It's important to recognize that just because you developed an ingenious idea or product doesn't mean that you can turn it into a successful business. It takes more than gathering some capital, renting an office or storefront, hanging out a sign, and waiting for customers to discover you.

What to Do

Consider hiring an expert to manage your business for you, or seek assistance from a consulting firm. Sit at the person's right elbow until you learn the fine details of operating a business.

If you can't justify the cost of an outsider, then take a class in management at your local community college or university. Meanwhile, until you've mastered your own successful management style, focus on some basic principles of what makes a company succeed and what positions it best for success:

◆ **Study the success of others.** Successful companies ask a lot of questions and adapt good ideas whenever they can.

◆ **Study your competition.** Why are they more successful or better known? What do they do that you should do, too? How can you do it better? What can you do differently?

◆ **Gather and analyze information in four areas strategic to your business.** The four areas are: finances, customers (develop a profile), your industry (what others are doing and how), and your market (what the market trends are).

◆ **Know who your best customers are.** Treat them accordingly.

◆ **Hire professional help.** Find help in highly specialized areas, such as accounting and law.

◆ **Use the best tools available.** Buy or lease computers, fax machines, software programs, telephone and messaging systems, or whatever serves your company best.

◆ **Solicit suggestions from employees.** Empower them to solve problems, and encourage them to find ways to make your operations better.

◆ **Give your employees what they need to get their work done.** Then get out of their way. I have long been intrigued by how people cite legendary football coach Vince Lombardi as an example of exemplary management, so once, while working with a client in Green Bay, I visited the Packers' Hall of Fame and Museum to study him myself. Of course there are traits that he alone possessed that other coaches did not; but what I learned is that managers could learn a lot from watching almost any football coach. All they have to do is watch one game and they'll realize that the coach never plays the role of quarterback. He doesn't jump onto the field and play defense when the other team has the ball, either. Instead, he works in advance of the game, then remains on the sidelines while the game progresses, being available for consultation, motivation, and guidance. The point is that the business manager cannot do the work for his people; he has to provide them with guidance and training, and then let them alone to win the game.

♦ **Be a role model for employees.** When it comes to managing people, you will find that people generally do what you expect them to do. And the best way to let them know what you expect, other than telling them, is to show them; show them through your own actions and your own expectations of yourself. If you want to set standards for your staff to live by, then you have to practice what you preach. Like a parent, you can't do one thing and say another and still expect your kids to learn and live the values important to you.

Character building in a company begins at the top. When I supervised employees at a utility years ago, I had a sign over my desk that read: "To build a successful team, build it with character, not characters." The owner or manager of a small business must have good character and must look for the same in employees. I had an acquaintance call me up once all excited about the fact that he had just hired a prime employee. It seems that the person had left the employ of my friend's major competitor and brought with her complete insider information and a databank of customers. Not wanting to rain on my friend's parade or condemn the person before meeting her, I simply urged caution, which my friend shrugged off, convinced that he could keep her happy at his company. Sure enough, three months later, she was off again, with his company's vital information in hand, to seek employment elsewhere. It goes without saying that if employees will cheat, steal, or lie for you, then they'll just as easily do it to you. So as manager or owner, don't hire people with negative qualities, and don't display them yourself, because by doing so you're telling your employees that it's OK to have less than good character.

♦ **Be a boss, not a buddy.** This is an especially hard lesson for owners of small businesses to learn. After all, in the lean years of growth, there may be a lengthy period of time in which there are few employees. The tendency is to run the operation as one big happy family in which everyone gets special favors and exceptions and things are overlooked. The problem enters when the company experiences growth and new employees come on board. Suddenly, the boss wants to develop a "real" company, with new rules and practices and respect for hours and chains of command. Quite often the people who were there the earliest, for example clerical staff, are suddenly at the bottom of the ladder and have a hard time adjusting to the new rules and ways of interacting.

Likewise, some owners like to build camaraderie by being employees' friends, doing things in off-hours together. The problem here is that it can be hard for employees to make the transition from buddy the night before to employee the next morning. The best advice is to be a boss at all times.

◆ **Develop a good relationship with your banker.** Don't wait for a crisis before you shake hands with him for the first time.

◆ **Learn to network.** People want to do business with people they know. So get out there and meet people.

◆ **Learn how to compile and interpret financial reports.** These reports can tip you off to shifts in sales, embezzlement, and a host of other potentially damaging situations.

◆ **Concentrate on your niche, at what you do best.** Don't try to be all things to all people.

◆ **Stress benefits to your customers.** Concentrate on benefits, not the features of what you offer. Customers need to know immediately how they will benefit from your product/service and how it will improve their lives.

◆ **Be willing to do what it will take to improve.** Ask former customers why they left. Ask current customers why they stay. Ask potential customers what it will take to make a relationship happen.

◆ **Sharpen your marketing skills.** Marketing is learning by doing, so start doing! Study your price levels, your product offerings, your location relative to your customers and their daily routines, and your image and positioning in the market.

◆ **Eliminate waste.** Plan your spending in advance, and stick to your budget. If your budget and actual expenses don't match, then figure out where the money is going. Try to bring operating expenses down, perhaps to less than 20 percent of sales. Every dollar saved from current operating costs goes directly to your bottom line. Conversely, don't be afraid to spend in areas that will help you earn more. These are not wasteful costs but rather wise investments.

◆ **Know when it's time to make a change.** Maintaining your niche or unique selling position is only possible if you can respond to the changes going on in your market and in yourself; otherwise, you may find yourself caught in a crisis that you don't know how to extract yourself from. Look for telltale signs indicating that change is necessary:

—*Everywhere you turn, you find more and more competitors.* If other companies are encroaching on your industry, they might also be rendering your niche commonplace. You may have to make changes to emphasize different features of your product or service. For years, I operated a firm that specialized in crisis management planning for the nuclear industry. When that field became flooded with new consulting firms, I sought work with chemical and manufacturing industries, retail establishments, professional firms, and eventually small businesses. By the time my competitors had learned the skills necessary to advise these industries, too, I had exhausted my desire to do the work any longer anyway. So I readily switched gears again, but this time into a line of work that interested me more.

—*Your interests are out of sync with your business.* In the previous item, I mentioned that I had a desire to change my work. It happens to business owners all the time. Knowing when to hold and when to fold can make the difference for success. Dedication does not necessarily mean fruitful work. If your heart's not in it, then you may be spinning your wheels. If you find that you are not as interested in your business as you used to be, change may be necessary. You can sell the company or, in some cases, simply close shop. If you don't want to close doors but do feel you need a break, then hire someone else to manage the business. Just be sure to hire people you can trust to make decisions without you.

—*Your customers are hooking up with your competition.* If you're convinced that they're not leaving because you did something wrong, then perhaps you didn't do something *right,* whereas your competition did. Find out what that something is, adopt it yourself, go one or two steps further

to provide even more value, then begin to court them back.
—*Your market disappears or your product no longer sells.* No matter what effort might have been expended in the '70s to save eight-track tapes and phonograph records, it wouldn't have been enough. Technology can create fickle markets for products. What's here today could be obsolete tomorrow. Your best bets are *not* to rely on one product and to stay abreast of industry trends and developments.

—*Your annual growth rate is stagnant.* Perhaps you and your employees have become complacent in seeking new customers. Maybe your marketing efforts are poorly targeted. Overhead expenses could be eating away at profits. Regardless, the trick is to identify the problem and make changes. When Marjorie Dunkel realized that her cost of doing business was increasingly eating into her profits, she devised a cost-control plan for her small Atlanta-based manufacturing company. Gas and electricity were rising steadily, and her water bill had increased by 50 percent during the past year. These increases made her aware of leaky pipes, poorly insulated walls, and inefficient lights. Basic repairs lowered her bills immediately. Then she turned to operational costs, such as long-distance telephone service and insurance policies. By threatening to switch, she got better rates. However, the threats worked only because she let service providers know that she was ready to make a change.

YOUR COMPANY IS LOSING CUSTOMERS

A LOSS OF CUSTOMERS CAN BE THE MOST DAMAGING CRISIS a company can experience, because without customers there is no business. Companies lose customers and clients for a variety of reasons—some that are within their control and some that are not. But those wise business owners who manage their companies with a focus on quality service and who are willing to make changes will find that most of their customers and clients will come back.

What to Do

Find out why your customers leave. According to the American Society for Quality (formerly the American Society of

Quality Control), here are the main reasons companies lose customers and clients:

- 68 percent are dissatisfied with a company representative's attitude of indifference
- 14 percent are dissatisfied with the product
- 9 percent are lured away by competition
- 5 percent are influenced by a friend to go elsewhere
- 3 percent move away
- 1 percent die

Because more than two-thirds of the problems (68 percent) result from employee interactions with customers, you should do the following:

- Make it a point to learn how employees treat customers
- Observe employee-customer interactions
- Ask employees what-if questions regarding customer requests
- Train them if you're not satisfied with the answers
- Move or fire employees who display indifference or an unwillingness to "serve" a customer

You may even want to do these things:

- Give employees subtitles that emphasize service. Have these titles printed on plaques that employees keep at their desks as reminders. For example, your receptionist could have a plaque for only her to see reading "Director of First Impressions." Your office manager could be "Director of Complaint Solicitations." Your floor supervisor could be referred to as the "Manager of Customer Satisfaction." What's the point? To impress upon employees how vital their work is to getting and keeping customers and clients.
- Provide incentives and rewards for the employees who are the most successful in keeping your customers happy.
- Finally, identify angry customers and work with them directly. They can cost your company a lot of money when they talk to friends and neighbors about their negative experiences. You may have to eat a little humble pie, but deal with the issue immediately. Talk to them, ask them what it will take to make them happy again, and then give them a peace offering with a built-in incentive to return, such as a discount on a future purchase.

YOU SUFFER FROM POOR CASH FLOW

THE BEST SURVIVAL TECHNIQUE FOR MANY BUSINESSES
could well be maintaining a positive cash flow. Without it, your business will not be able to weather the finicky sales environment. You might have one month with high sales, then two or three months with less revenue than expenses. If you can't maintain the cash flow from the sales in the first month, you may not make it through the second or third months, and certainly not into the fourth and fifth months.

David Platner (not his real name) experienced what every business owner dreams of—a growing business. His Florida-based custom-furniture-making business was picking up new clients every day, and orders were increasing. Initially he didn't think things could be better. That is, until he realized that not only were his orders increasing but so too were his expenses. As a result, the money wasn't coming in fast enough, and he began to experience problems with cash flow.

The importance of cash flow cannot be emphasized enough. In fact, it's not just a problem of small businesses. The Chrysler Corporation, whose sales numbered in the billions of dollars, was hit by a frightening cash crisis right in the midst of a recession. The federal government provided substantial financial support to keep it afloat.

 What to Do

Perform a realistic cash flow projection so that you have enough cash resources to fulfill the tasks you have outlined in your business plan. Cut costs where you can. Make changes in collecting your accounts receivable. Don't get so caught up in production and marketing that you overlook invoicing and collections. If it takes ninety days to collect on a big account, and you need to pay your own bills within two weeks, you'll find your self in deep trouble.

While doing that cash flow project, conduct a thorough assessment of your cash flow cycle (the time that transpires from when you spend your money on raw materials through the time you are paid by your customers). You may find that you are financing your product for too lengthy a period of time. In this case, you will have to

- ◆ **Collect payment from your customers more quickly.**
  Don't hurt yourself by financing other people.
- ◆ **Move your product faster.** The faster your inventory turns over, the better.
- ◆ **Pay your bills more slowly.** However, don't miss deadlines; you may have to pay late charges if you don't pay on time. Renegotiate your payment dates, if possible. And while you're at it, discuss the possibility of volume discounts.

  You may also help your cash flow if you

- ◆ **Take people off your payroll who do not earn their keep.**
- ◆ **Find less-expensive sources of supplies, as long as the quality doesn't change.**
- ◆ **Move to a less-expensive address.**
- ◆ **Postpone buying equipment that is bigger and more powerful than what you need right now.**
- ◆ **And finally, establish good credit.** It will be your cushion when you experience financial setbacks and poor cash flow. But establishing good credit takes advance work, and the reason is clear: Lenders want to know about you and your business *before* you need to borrow money. Before needing the money, you need to have convinced lenders that you are a viable commercial venture worthy of loans. To establish a positive relationship with a lender, choose one that has a small-business lending officer. Why waste time with a loan institution that does not have a history of making small-business loans? Get to know the people who work there. Make them aware of what your business is all about.

Always shop around before getting a loan. Rates and conditions vary almost daily, and you want to find the best terms available at the time you request a loan. Also, find the right type of loan for your business and your situation. This will be determined by how much money you need, for how long, and how much you can afford to pay for it.

If you approach a bank for a loan, don't ask for a minimum amount that will let you squeak by; instead, ask for a realistic amount so that you won't have to go back again.

Another option is to seek a "microloan" that is backed by the Small Business Administration. These loans were initially created for businesses that have trouble obtaining conventional loans, and they generally carry a limit of $25,000. For more information, contact your local SBA office (see resources).

YOU NEED A LOAN—AND QUICKLY!

YOU NEED FUNDING IMMEDIATELY, AND YOU HAVEN'T LAID the groundwork in advance (as described above) to attain a business loan on short notice. What can you do now?

What to Do

Unless you have a wealthy friend or angel who believes in your company or devoted employees who are willing to invest, you will have to consider personal sources of funding. Can you:

- Convert personal items or resources into cash?
- Take out a second mortgage?
- Secure a home-equity loan?
- Get a loan against the cash value of your life insurance policy?
- Tap into a credit union?
- Withdraw money from a retirement plan? (Be wary of what this will do to your taxes.)
- Pay bills with credit cards? (Watch for high interest rates.)
- Borrow from friends and relatives? (Watch out. Sometimes the emotional paybacks can be tougher than high interest rates from more traditional sources.)
- Negotiate with a long-standing customer for an early payment on a future large order?
- Discuss some creative financing options and payment schedules with suppliers and vendors?

Regardless of what you choose, remember that this situation may well be a turning point for your company. You need to determine not only what will happen if you do not get the money but what will happen if you do. If you resort to credit cards, are you setting yourself up to rely on quick loans and quick fixes that in the long run—due to high interest rates—will put you in worse standing than where you were before you got the money? If you negotiate with vendors for creative financing—for example, offering to pay more for their goods if they will wait until you've been paid by customers—can you ensure this remains confidential so that the vendor doesn't spread the word that you're in dire straits? The point is, there can be repercussions for using all the forms of financing outlined above.

YOUR BUSINESS IS BUILT AROUND ONE PRODUCT

IF YOU OFFER ONLY ONE PRODUCT, YOU MAY BE HEADED FOR disaster. It's no secret that the key to success in any business is to sell products or services to repeat customers. If you rely on one product, you may find yourself vulnerable when your competition begins to take over the market or the demand for your product changes.

 What to Do

Build and maintain a catalog or portfolio of related products to sell to your customers over and over again. Think in terms of markets rather than products. Once your market starts buying from you, make sure you have other products to offer them. If you are selling a service, make sure that it is a service they can use over and over again. For example, I mentioned earlier that I used to own and manage a crisis management consulting firm. After being contracted by an organization to conduct an assessment of its ability to weather and manage a crisis, we would establish a comprehensive response program. One of the benefits we offered was that we provided the company with a program that it could maintain itself. Accordingly, we developed the program to work with its systems, procedures, location, and personnel. Then we trained employees to keep it updated. However, to ensure that we were able to turn each client into a repeat customer, we also provided development of exercises or simulations that would test the programs and their personnel under simulated situations. It is important to outsource scenario and exercise development, because allowing employees to develop their own exercise would be like allowing a student to assign his own grade in school: there's no objectivity. Thus, clients used our service again and again.

YOU HAVE AN IDEA YOU WANT TO IMPLEMENT

TO STAY AHEAD OF YOUR COMPETITORS, YOU HAVE TO BE creative. You have to develop new products and come up with new ideas. After all, everyone knows that ideas can only help a company, not hurt it, right? Wrong. Ask the folks at Coca-Cola what a bad idea did to them in 1985. Remember New Coke? Remember how, as a result of that product, Coke lost market share to its largest competitor, Pepsi? The introduction of New Coke has been recorded in Coca-Cola history as one of the most damaging crises it has ever experienced and, at the time, a negative turning point for the company.

What to Do

How can you tell whether an idea is a good one without wasting a lot of time and money on it? The answer is to do a lot of thinking, research, and talking with employees, members of your board of directors, and anyone else with a vested interest in your company. Determine:

◆ What would be the contribution to the company's performance if the idea were implemented?

◆ Does the idea help with any other areas of the business?

◆ Will the idea help the company to reach its objectives?

◆ Is the idea in line with the company's mission?

◆ If anything stands in the way of implementing the idea, can you move or eliminate the impediment without creating new problems?

◆ Do your employees like the new idea?

◆ Do you have—or can you get with little outlay of cash—the resources needed to implement the idea?

◆ Will the idea make immediate sense to onlookers and customers, or will you have to spend a lot of money in education?

◆ Can you set up a system to test the idea in advance? Depending upon your product or service, you might want to do a beta test by offering a service for free for a short time or setting up a consumer testing group to try the product.

If you determine the idea has value, then proceed accordingly, but keep a cautious eye on the progress. According to blind taste tests, consumers preferred the taste of New Coke to original Coke by a wide margin. Yet when New Coke was brought to market, the result was massive consumer rejection, attributed by consumer analysts to consumers' resistance to change. So proceed cautiously as you test-market your idea or product, as described next.

YOU NEED TO TEST-MARKET YOUR IDEA OR PRODUCT

WE ALL COME UP WITH WHAT WE CONSIDER TO BE A GREAT idea from time to time. Unfortunately, that doesn't mean that everyone else will think it's a great idea, too, or if they do, that they will buy it. We've also seen ideas that were surprising successes even though they looked like potential bombs from the outset—for example, the Pet Rock phenomenon of the '70s. And, in fact, the Pet Rock is a classic example that hopeful entrepreneurs point to when they want to justify their ideas without any testing, saying, "If people will buy a Pet Rock, they'll buy anything." But this thinking is illogical, because the Pet Rock obviously offered at least one benefit to consumers that no other product did. It's hard to know exactly what that benefit was; and if you ask a dozen people, you'll get a dozen answers, from "It made me laugh" to "It was the perfect gift for someone who has everything." Regardless, you can't assume the success of one unusual item will assure the success of another, even if all other factors—such as advertising and distribution—are equal.

What to Do

◆ **Produce samples of the product.** The first drawback in test-marketing is the fact that you actually have to produce some of your new product. Asking a consumer how they would like a product if it did X, Y, and Z is not the same as placing it in their hands and letting them *see* it do X, Y, and Z. Remember: people don't always do as they say, meaning that people can assure you they will buy your product but then won't do it when the product becomes available. Your chances of their following through on their words increase if they give this same promise while looking at or using the real thing, rather than a sketch or description.

◆ **Try to sell it.** The next challenge is attempting to sell the product without eating up your advertising budget. That's why you often encounter companies doing taste tests and demonstrating products at shopping malls. These companies literally go to the people and put their product in their faces. But the problem with merely providing taste tests as opposed to selling jars of the product is that people tend to accept almost anything for free. You put a spoonful of new jelly in their mouths and they'll ooh and aah and comment on its terrific taste, but that doesn't mean they'll buy it when it appears on the supermarket shelves. By then, they might forget it was the delicious product they sampled, disagree with the selling price, or be turned off by its packaging.

◆ **Survey; ask questions.** Of course, not every product can be created for test-marketing. Sometimes the prices are just too prohibitive. In this case, you'll have to rely on questions such as these:

—Do you like the product?

—What would you be willing to pay for it if it were conveniently available in a retail location?

—Would you buy it if it were available at the price you quoted?

—If you were shopping for this product, where would you expect to be able to find it?

—What similar product are you using now (if appropriate), and how is this one different?

—Is the difference a good feature or a bad feature?

—If good, would you switch to the new product? Why?

As you sell your product or ask your questions, be sure to learn as much as you can about the demographics (age, sex, race, education, occupation, income, etc.) of your audience. This will come in handy later for marketing efforts.

Why would test-marketing a product be a potential turning point for your company? The biggest reason is that if the product is an unprecedented hit, you may have to move quickly to bring it to market before competitors produce a clone. Another reason is that unless you test-market appropriately, you may get answers that will convince you of a product's success, but then when it's brought to market—tens of thousands of dollars later— you find out otherwise. Through any test-marketing endeavor, seek outside objectivity and guidance from professionals unattached to the product and your dreams for it. You might even want to engage the services of a profes-sional test-marketing organization.

YOU ARE BEING THREATENED WITH A HOSTILE TAKEOVER

YOU'RE EXCITED: BUSINESS IS DOING VERY WELL. SO WELL, in fact, that it has caught the attention of others. Others in higher places. Suddenly you get the word that another com-pany has informed the SEC of its intention to acquire a large number of your shares for the purpose of eventual takeover.

What to Do

First, you'll need to determine whether this news is good or bad. It could be that the terms of the acquisition will be attractive, that your position and those of your employees in the new company will be secure, and that your company will be positioned for new growth.

If, however, this is not something you want to have hap-pen because it could spell the end of your company as you know it, then you may have a fight on your hands.

Fortunately, quite often when the other company learns that you are not interested in merging and intend to fight the takeover, they will back off because they're not interested in a long and costly battle.

Meanwhile, circle your wagons:

◆ Meet with your board, get their support to fight the takeover, and outline your plan of attack.

◆ Form a response team and make assignments.

◆ Get legal staff on board, and assign them the task of identify-ing any regulatory roadblocks that could delay the takeover, so that they will have more time to identify any legal techni-calities that could prevent the takeover.

◆ Refuse to meet with your competitors (and don't let anyone else in your company meet with them, either), lest they get a heads-up on what you plan to do.

◆ Repurchase enough shares of your stock to prevent the other company from gaining a controlling interest.

◆ Make changes to your company that would discourage the other company's plans, such as altering your bylaws.

◆ Tell everyone important to you and your business why you think the takeover would be a bad move and why you intend to fight it. You never know what resources they may have at their disposal in a crisis. Imagine a supportive banker arranging enough funding for your company to raise the price of your stock, making it impossible for the other company to even consider a takeover.

◆ Divest your company of the features that make it attractive to the other company so that it is less likely to pursue takeover.

◆ Meet with financial and legal counsel regularly to discuss your options.

YOU KEEP MAKING COSTLY MISTAKES IN ADVERTISING

WE'VE ALL HEARD THE SAYING THAT ADVERTISING PAYS, but we just don't know which part. What this means to a small business is that you might spend a lot of money in advertising only to have it come up short of your expectations. In fact, I have seen at least two small businesses enter a crisis because their expensive advertising efforts fell short, leaving them with a large inventory and little cash.

What to Do

Be realistic. Just because an ad costs a lot of money doesn't mean it's any more effective than one that costs much less. Being familiar with a few aspects of advertising might save you from making costly mistakes:

◆ Find out who your prospects are. Conduct a survey. Have customers complete business reply cards, which you hand out generously in the store or send to their homes. Get the names of people who have purchased from you in the past. Once you develop a profile, tailor your ads to their tastes and interests and the medium of their choice.

◆ Don't concentrate on what your company has to offer. Instead, make your advertisement read as though you offer solutions for your prospects. Don't think in terms of features; instead emphasize benefits.

◆ Get your prospects' attention by talking directly to them, not to the mass market. Tell them what it costs them to ignore your message. Use a headline that states the problem and alludes to the benefit that is to come. Then add a subhead that provides the solution. For example, headline: "Stop spending too much money on designer suits"; subhead: "Shop at Paul's Place and get more for less".

◆ Give prospects a reason to act now, while they're thinking about you. Give them a limited-time offer, a two-for-one sale, a number to call for a discount, a bonus for buying today.

◆ Use testimonials. People don't trust ads as much as they trust the positive experience of a satisfied customer.

◆ Offer a guarantee of satisfaction. If you remove the risk of buying, prospects will be more inclined to give it a try.

◆ Ask for success stories of any agency you employ to coordinate advertising for you. Be skeptical. Challenge their thinking. Ask them what consumer research they base their work on. Ask for a money-back guarantee, or at least a percentage of your money back if the advertising does not produce the results the agency promised it would.

YOU NEED TO PUT THE MOTION IN PROMOTION

YOU'VE BUILT A SOLID COMPANY THAT OFFERS A VALUABLE service. You're so busy, in fact, that you can't take on any more clients right now. And as for marketing, well, you're convinced it's not necessary right now because your agenda is full and your current clients will probably refer others to you down the road.

This scenario is a disaster waiting to happen. I learned the hard way in years of consulting that when you are at your busiest serving clients is exactly the time when you should be beefing up your marketing effort. Your promotion should always be in motion. Why? Because all good things come to an end eventually. Contracts expire, clients redirect their focus or cut back, industry trends change, technology makes something obsolete, and on and on. Being too busy today to market for tomorrow will come back to haunt you.

What to Do

◆ Market your business all the time. Always be available to talk about your company and its products or services. Keep planning new and creative promotional strategies. And promote your product wisely, doing everything you can to make your potential customers identify with your product. One marketing axiom says that you should "Sell the sizzle, not the steak." In other words, highlight the benefits or the perceived value to customers, not the features you offer. If you are trying to sell a car, for example, what you sell is a safe, enjoyable, reliable, and perhaps glamorous excursion on the open road, not a mound of metal, glass, bolts, and rubber that were put together in a particular way.

◆ And, of course, while you are courting new prospects, keep trying to win back the old ones, and surpass the expectations of the current ones. Also be sure to make your clients aware of the full range of your services. If they're happy with what you're doing in one area, they will be more inclined to consider you for another area over a company with whom they have no experience. And finally, use your satisfied clients for testimonials and referrals. Tell them that you want to work with more people or companies just like them.

YOU EXPERIENCE SUPPLY PROBLEMS

IF YOUR SUPPLIER EXPERIENCES A CRISIS, THEN CHANCES are you might, too. After all, if suppliers can't keep up with demand, you might fall behind on orders. Likewise, if your product receives unexpected attention and sales soar, then you may find that you're tapping into your suppliers for more than they were prepared to handle.

What to Do

◆ Get to know your suppliers. If you don't think they can keep pace with your growth, then find new or backup sources. Present them with what-if situations to see how they respond. Determine whether their thinking is realistic.

Sure, a wise management step would be to have everything in writing, but that's not fail-safe. If a supplier is in trouble, a breach of contract is just one more item on the list, whereas it will be a crisis for you.

A RECESSION IS COMING

AS I WRITE THIS, PREDICTIONS OF A RECESSION ARE ALL OVER the map. Depending upon whom you listen to, a major recession is going to hit next month, by Christmas, within two years, or not within the foreseeable future. As with everything else in this book, prudent management dictates that you give advance thought to how you will handle a recession when it hits. Instead of making recession planning a time of worry, turn it into a chance to identify ways to survive and thrive.

Planning for a recession can actually open the eyes of some small businesses to the amount of fat they carry unnecessarily, thus giving them a chance to streamline operations before it's even necessary. The result? A healthier company for good and bad times.

What to Do

◆ Don't deny the possibility that it could happen to you. During a recession, the economy gets smaller. Business activity goes down as people look for ways to save money and spend less. Unless your product or service is a staple for your customers, you will probably feel the effects of this decreased spending.

◆ Secure financing now. Make sure your credit lines are in place with good terms.

◆ Reduce your overhead costs. Make repairs to lower bills, negotiate contracts at lower rates, and shop around for better rates on service plans and insurance policies. Every company struggles with creeping expenses, and it gets worse during periods of prolonged economic growth.

◆ Rethink how you'll turn a profit. If, for example, your business sells high-ticket bikes, you may find sales going down as consumers try to keep their current bikes in good condition and on the road. What this means is that there will be a larger market for parts. Figure out how you can turn that into your profit center during the recession.

◆ Diversify your sources of revenue. Don't rely on just one product or service to get you through a recession.

YOUR LOCATION ISN'T WORKING FOR YOU

THE MANTRA IN REAL ESTATE IS "LOCATION, LOCATION, location." The same is true for many small businesses. Unfortunately, the wrong location or the wrong lease on that location can cause it to be a money pit.

What to Do

◆ **Choose the right location.** Regardless of your line of business, location is important to the image you're trying to create. Generally, the company that can deliver the goods the fastest, least-expensive way will get the contract. If you operate a consulting firm and your clients are spread throughout the country, you can offer significantly lower prices if you live near a major airport, because it won't cost the client as much money to get you to their offices. If you plan to set up a shop to manufacture a product, you will want to consider your accessibility to suppliers and transportation methods to reach customers. Shipping charges can add up quickly. If you're looking for a shop that customers will visit, then you should do a careful demographic study of population statistics, labor force availability, per capita income, education level, and other important statistical information available from the library, the chamber of commerce, or census records.

If you're thinking of leasing a facility for a business with customer traffic, do a careful study of that space first. Sure, there may be a busy grocery store located two stores down from where you want to set up shop, but if that's the store drawing the crowds, you may be out of luck. Buyers won't put their groceries in their cars and then shop leisurely for items like computers, vacation packages, and wallpaper. Besides, who feels like spending more money after they've seen their grocery bill? You should decide if a grocery storefront is in line with the buying disposition you want in your customers. For card shops and drugstores, it usually is.

◆ **Choose the right lease.** A lease may seem like a simple document, but bear in mind that it's also a legal document, so study it carefully before you sign it. Your business will suffer greatly from the wrong location. In addition to the length of the lease and the rent, it should spell out other terms, such as the following:

—How much can the rent go up, and under what circumstances?

—Can you sublease any of your space?

—What services, such as electricity, heating, cleaning, and snow removal, are covered?

—Who pays for improvements?

—Who pays for insurance?

You have the right to *request* that additional details be added to the lease too, such as:

— no competitors being allowed to move into the building or adjacent offices

—a standard nondisturbance clause in case the landlord goes bankrupt

YOU HAVE INFORMATION THAT COULD BENEFIT YOUR COMPETITION

PICK UP ANY MAGAZINE ABOUT SMALL BUSINESS AND YOU will invariably come across an article about a former small business owner whose winning idea or product was copied by a competitor and delivered to the mass market before he had a chance to succeed. Unfortunately, too many people don't appropriately safeguard their knowledge.

Another problem is that the Internet makes it so easy to share information. Businesses are being encouraged to do so by the news media and digital consultants, all of whom are hyping the changes in the "new economy." Share information, share technology, and everyone benefits, according to these techno-wizards. Or do they? By sharing information, you might just risk losing your competitive edge.

Whether you're an employer, a small business owner and entrepreneur, an artist, or an employee, it's smart to take steps to protect your intellectual property: that stuff we know, create, invent, draw, write, speak, think up, learn, discover, and compile; anything that is valuable to the way we do business and that could be valuable to other people.

You might produce intellectual property yourself, or you might purchase it or hire someone else to produce it for you. Regardless of how you get it, the point is that it is important for the progress of your business, and therefore it should be protected.

To protect those who take the time to offer progress to our society, laws have evolved. Different forms of protection for intellectual property include copyrights, patents, trademarks, and trade secrets. Find out more about each by talking to an attorney or contacting the SBA (see resources). Unfortunately, most of these options take time. You still need a means by which to protect yourself as you await the approval of intellectual-property safeguards such as copyrights and trademarks.

What to Do

Develop and use nondisclosure agreements. You can find basic forms in many office supply stores, or talk to an attorney.

Having an individual sign a nondisclosure agreement will allow you to disclose your intellectual property to him without fear that he will then share the information with someone else or use it to benefit himself in any way. You should use such an agreement even if you're just trying to solicit investors in your business.

SURVIVAL IS THREATENED BECAUSE A PRINCIPAL OR PARTNER WANTS TO LEAVE

IT'S HARD TO IMAGINE EVER WANTING TO LEAVE THE business you've loved and built for years, but it does happen. Partners, principal players, or others with some form of financial control and clout may someday announce that they want out. People change unexpectedly. Situations change. Society changes. My partner in my first company decided he wanted out after almost nine years of operating our service business. His announcement didn't surprise me. We had both admitted boredom with the company and had been discussing changing our focus and our services and exploring new areas. What did surprise me, however, was the depth to which he sought a change: He actually moved out of the country to seek employment. During the process of closing up the company, I discovered that we hadn't included a workable exit system into our business arrangement, which meant that if I had wanted to continue the company, I might have been faced with figuring out how to buy him out. No doubt this would have led to animosity, delays, interruption of services with clients, and low cash flow. Frankly, with no structure or agreed-upon exit procedure to fall back on or to make my partner adhere to, I don't know if the company could have survived at that point anyway. I was lucky to be as desirous of a professional change as he was.

What to Do

First of all, business partnerships are a lot like love—if one wants out, the other has got to let go. A partner who is shamed, threatened, or talked into staying will not stay for long, because that person's heart is no longer in the business. And you can't assume that the individual you've worked with and trusted for years will show the same integrity in the end. When someone wants out, they think only of themselves, not what came before. Unfortunately, what too few business owners realize is that the need for change would be better served with some time off or away from the business rather than with a quick or precipitous permanent arrangement— because once you're out, you can't go back.

A partner's potential exit is just one more reason to incorporate your business, but even that will not protect you fully. My partner and I were incorporated, so buying him out would not have been a problem, but what if his departure had been untimely for the business, and what if I had wanted the business to go on? For these reasons and more, you should factor a workable exit system into your partnering and business agreements.

YOU HAVEN'T INSURED YOURSELF ADEQUATELY

IF YOU'RE LIKE ME, THE CHECKS YOU FIND HARDEST TO write or authorize are those to an insurance company. Buying insurance is no fun—it costs too much and takes money away from other plans I have for my company. I am much more interested in building something than I am in protecting against its loss.

It seems that I'm not alone. According to a September

1999 *Entrepreneur* magazine subscriber survey, only 55 percent of the respondents believed they had "adequate" insurance for property damage, fire, theft, and liability—the essentials.

Quite bluntly, you're flirting with disaster if you don't have adequate coverage. This book gives you hundreds of tips and insights on preparing for and handling the unexpected. With this advice, you'll be able to avoid or eliminate many potential crises altogether; however, there's always that unexpected situation you fail to anticipate. If you have no insurance, could you afford to fight a racial discrimination or sexual harassment lawsuit when even a baseless accusation can cost you $50,000 and more? Do you realize that home insurance won't necessarily cover your home office equipment if you experience a fire or flood? And where will the money come from if you send an employee out to pick up a box of donuts for the board meeting and en route he gets into an accident that ends up in a lawsuit against you?

Also, be aware that all disasters are not covered automatically by the "standard" insurance policy. Your exposures need to be identified through a vulnerability assessment (Chapter 1), and the policy needs to be tailored to address these exposures. Then you can offset potential losses by purchasing insurance coverage for these identified perils. Learn more about insurance options in Chapter 6.

What to Do

Fortunately, the growth of small businesses has brought with it the growth of new insurance products to choose from. And competition is stronger than ever in the insurance industry, so getting a better price than what you've gotten in the past is a real possibility.

Identify a qualified insurance agent you want to work with and together develop a comprehensive insurance plan. Show him the results of your Vulnerability Assessment, as discussed in Chapter 1, and then let him know what you're doing to eliminate risks. It could be that many of your efforts will result in a better price for you. For example, farms, ranches, and nurseries are considered small businesses and are especially vulnerable to fires. These businesses can lower their fire insurance rates by simply putting a pond on the property.

When you've got the agent's recommendations and prices, check with another agent. Compare the prices and the coverage. The second agent may identify something the first agent overlooked.

Your Worst Threat: A Smoldering Crisis

IT'S A MISTAKE TO ASSUME THAT MOST ORGANIZATIONAL crises arise from accidents and other catastrophes, according to Larry Smith, president of the Institute for Crisis Management in Louisville, Kentucky (www.crisisexperts.com). Smith's institute researches and catalogs business-crisis news stories into a database, which has analyzed almost 65,000 stories since 1990.

"Most crises, regardless of the size of the company involved, are neither accidental nor sudden," Smith explains. "Instead, they are smoldering crises, accounting for approximately two-thirds of the crises experienced by companies of all sizes." And he says they generally involve questionable, illegal, unethical, or irresponsible activity by someone within the organization, frequently involving other members of the organization or people who routinely interact with organizational personnel.

Not only do these smoldering problems go unaddressed, according to Smith, but also someone in the organization is usually aware of or has neglected symptoms of them. So the crisis comes not from lack of knowledge, but from unwillingness to report or deal with unpleasant realities. Much of the problem, then, can be attributed to management.

"Our research suggests that the vast majority of crises are caused by the actions—or inactions—of managers, not employees or outside agents," he says, citing 75 percent of business crises as being attributable directly or indirectly to management. (An example of indirect responsibility would be a sexual harassment case in which the harassment is primarily to blame, but management's failure to address it is secondarily at fault.) "Next in line are employees, who cause roughly 14 percent, with the remaining 11 percent caused by 'acts of God' or agents external to the organization (i.e., terrorists, activists, competitors, disgruntled customers).

"The result," Smith says, "is that what may have been a controllable business problem—had the owners or management recognized and dealt with the crisis—now turns into an uncontrolled business crisis. By this, I mean that the problem has escaped the organization and will then be covered by the media and investigated by government and judicial agencies."

As a result, these smoldering crises have even greater potential for threatening the profitability and even the existence of a small business than do sudden crises, according to Smith.

"In a sudden crisis, the public, news organizations, and government officials know that the organizations' owners or managers are not to blame for the situation. In fact, business owners might even receive a degree of sympathy and support during the first few days," he explains. "However, if it is a smoldering crisis—one he should have identified and attended to earlier—then the worm turns immediately on him when the information comes to light. And it will, during the course of an investigation or a series of hearings after the event. The question on everyone's mind will be 'How could you have allowed this to happen?'"

The end result could be damaging, or at least embarrassing, to a company when it's revealed that the owners or managers tolerated or allowed illegal practices with the books, shoddy workmanship, inaccurate reporting to the government, unfair hiring practices, discriminatory practices, and on and on. Smith says that due to the prolonged duration of smoldering crises, they also

◆ drain dollars over long periods of time away from the principal business activity

◆ divert management and employee attention from the central activity of the organization

◆ undermine customer confidence in the ability of the organization to perform its primary function—providing goods or services

Finally, Smith points out that small business owners can locate and resolve smoldering problems before they flare into uncontrollable crises if they create a climate of openness in the organization. "Thousands of crises are prevented every year because business owners remain astute and because they do some advance planning to be prepared in case a crisis does hit," he says.

Managing Means Thinking Ahead

AS A MANAGER, MUCH OF YOUR JOB IS TO THINK THROUGH possible problems before they hit. The following list includes some important questions that will help you plan ahead.

- ◆ Have you identified and removed as much risk as possible from all aspects of your business?
- ◆ Are you alert to, or able to detect, smoldering crises at the earliest possible moment?
- ◆ Do your employees feel free to bring you disgruntlements and bad news?
- ◆ Do you take their concerns seriously?
- ◆ Are you open to sudden opportunities and quick change?
- ◆ Will your employees easily accept change as well?
- ◆ Have you formed plans and a team to deal with unexpected situations and crises?
- ◆ Have you trained your employees to use these plans?
- ◆ Have you planned for all the administrative aspects of a crisis (Where will we meet? Who will serve as spokesperson? Who will need to be called? Where can we get more help?), so that you are free to concentrate on the content of the crisis?
- ◆ Have you thought through how you will marshal your resources when adversity hits?
- ◆ Have you planned where your team will meet during a crisis? Have you equipped that location with as many resources as possible?

CHAPTER 4

Practice the Personnel Touch with Employees

ANY BUSINESS OWNERS WHO have a small staff think they are not vulnerable to the disastrous situations that strike corporations whose workforces number in the thousands. After all, with employees relatively close to the employer, complaints and misunderstandings can be addressed at once, rather than being sent to a committee. However, it's not just employee grievances that can cause the downfall of a business, as shown by the two following stories.

"One day, out of the blue, Duane—my most trusted and necessary employee—came to me and announced that he was leaving to start his own business," says Karen Alderman (not her real name), CEO of a Miami-based public relations firm. "And as if that wasn't damaging enough, his company now competes directly with mine, *and* he took my two most profitable clients."

As Alderman explains it, she taught, nurtured, supported, and confided in this employee; yet in one move, years of experience walked out the door, and several important clients with him.

Alderman admits that she had searched months for an ambitious and competent employee to help build her business to its staff of seven employees and twenty-four steady clients. She was thrilled to have found Duane five years ago. But now that he's left, not only are her feelings hurt, so is her bottom line. The two clients that Duane took with him accounted for 42 percent of her revenue. She was forced to let two employees go. When she did that, three other clients switched to Duane, who in turn hired one of Alderman's former employees for his company. Preventive lawyering—with its annoying and time-consuming contracts and noncompete agreements—might not have completely eliminated this risk, but it could have done a lot to control it.

Buz Fosbaugh, on the other hand, had devoted employees—perhaps *too* devoted. When one of his storage buildings caught on fire and subsequently exploded, slightly injuring one employee, it drew the attention of the local newspaper, since the structure, part of his commercial nursery, was next to a residential development.

Because Fosbaugh was not in town when the fire occurred, a well-meaning employee attempted to "save" Fosbaugh's reputation. She told an inquisitive reporter that the explosion could not have been prevented because, in order to keep the employees safe, Fosbaugh stored all the "dangerous" chemicals, fertilizers, and pesticides in the building that burned and that only Fosbaugh was allowed to go in there. Further investigation by the intrigued reporter revealed that Buz did not have permits to store such materials and that he probably would not have gotten permission anyway since the building was so close to a residential neighborhood.

Additionally, many people who saw the story on the 6 P.M. news that night inferred from the news coverage that the entire nursery had burned to the ground. As Fosbaugh explains it, "One of those listeners was the machinery supplier for my landscaping service. After he tried calling me at home but wasn't able to reach me, he panicked and called another customer who had eyed the tractor he had specially ordered for me. The tractor sold before I was even back in town. As a result, I was not able to complete six major landscaping jobs for clients, all of whom eventually canceled their contracts." With his financial situation already in jeopardy, Fosbaugh saw the end of his business when he received a hefty fine from the Environmental Protection Agency for not reporting that he stored large quantities of hazardous materials. He ended up closing his doors completely.

Employees are a blessing and a headache for entrepreneurs and small business owners. After all, when it comes to your business, the old adage applies: "If you want to grow, you've got to let go." Most business owners think that this means only letting go of duties and responsibilities. They don't find out until too late that it means turning over control of many aspects of their business to employees.

With employees can come a long list of potentially unexpected events and legal problems: product tampering, contamination, sabotage, sexual harassment, workplace violence, theft, claims of discrimination, defamatory gossip, snooping, whistle-blowing, hiring and firing fiascos, costly health and safety programs, strikes, and demonstrations, to name a few. Even something as seemingly innocuous as a petty disagreement between two employees can destroy morale. Poor morale then can become evident to customers. Few customers want to patronize an establishment or give vital work to a business that is filled with tension.

Even if your business is affected by an unexpected event that was *not* initiated by an employee, you may still find that your responsibility to your workforce is heavy. Keeping track of employees and their needs can be a daunting task for any overburdened entrepreneur. You may have to

- communicate policy decisions and information about the crisis to employees;
- locate replacement workers;
- provide trauma and psychological counseling for employees and families;
- ensure that health care benefits are processed quickly; and
- address employee concerns regarding longevity of the organization—all while you're attempting to continue operating your business.

In this chapter you will learn the principal ways that employees can render a small company vulnerable and how you can act now to avoid crises in the future. Statistically, small companies are less likely to experience sabotage or strikes than their larger competitors, but it's the smaller incidents—such as employee theft, poor customer service, and improper hiring practices—that can put a small company under or damage its reputation.

Tackling Employee Issues

DO YOU KNOW WHERE YOUR EMPLOYEES ARE?

AS BUSINESSES IN THE ALFRED P. MURRAH FEDERAL BUILDING
experienced after the Oklahoma City bombing, there may
come a time when you will have to evacuate your building.
What's more, even if everyone exits your building safely during an emergency, that doesn't mean your troubles are over.
Following the bombing, many employees called family
members and friends to pick them up. Lack of communication resulted in rescue workers wasting time and other family members suffering unneeded anxiety over loved ones who
were already safe. The confusion hampered the ability of
each organization in that building to set up temporary offices
elsewhere in an attempt to continue business.

Tom Benson (not his real name) of Benson's Auto
Repair near Pittsburgh knows all too well the importance
of employee accountability, even with his small staff of
three. One day while his employees were routinely working
on vehicles, the hydraulic lift failed, crashing to the garage
floor. As Benson explains, "We all thought Gary was under
that car. The last time any of us had seen him, he was
working on the brakes of a car on the lift. We panicked,
assumed the worst, and dialed 911. I was scared to death,
and I was wondering how in the world I was going to break
the news to his family." As it turned out, Gary had taken a
break to go to the bathroom and to run across the street to
grab lunch. After the fire truck and the ambulance got
there and everyone was anxiously considering how to proceed, Benson continues, "Gary came walking in the side
door, chewing on a burger and asking what all the commotion was about. Unfortunately, before Gary walked in, his
wife had called and one of my employees felt compelled to
tell her what we thought had happened. I don't think she's
ever forgiven us for scaring her like that. Add to that, we
got some bad press in the local paper about the whole
thing. Now, we're all careful to account for our where-
abouts at all times. I learned the hard way to make accountability a policy."

 **What to Do**

Make plans now to ensure accountability of all employees. More than one rescue worker has died from entering a burning building to find an employee who later was discovered elsewhere. Designate at least two meeting areas outside your building. One should be close by and the other farther away (but still within walking distance). Instruct each person how to take roll and to report in before leaving the area. Designate a meeting place across the street at another business, for example, and provide that business with periodic updates of your personnel lists and offer to keep the same for them in case they ever experience an emergency.

Don't forget guests, patients, and clients in your building during accountability. If possible, start a routine program whereby you require all visitors to register and record name, address, and phone number upon entry. Factor this entry ledger into your evacuation plans.

ARE YOUR EMPLOYEES SAFE?

YOU KNOW THAT OSHA STANDARDS DICTATE SAFE WORKING conditions for all companies, but you may not be sure how they apply to your business. Instead of poring through all the tedious government regulations and taking a chance on misinterpreting something you read and then facing potential fines, take action.

What to Do

If you're not sure whether your work environment would be considered safe by OSHA standards, then ask them. After all, they will be the ones to hand out any citations for safety violations, so it only makes sense to go directly to them. The effort will help you avoid penalties and keep your workers safe.

Many business owners are not aware that OSHA offers free consultations. When you request a consultation, you must commit to correcting any findings. Fortunately, if any problems are identified during the inspection, you are not cited and no penalties will be imposed. Instead, you will be given time to correct the problems.

Call or write OSHA for the handbook, *Consultation Services for the Employer* (OSHA publication #3047). You will find OSHA contact information in Resources.

ARE YOUR EMPLOYEES TRAINED APPROPRIATELY?

GENERALLY, WHEN AN EMPLOYEE MAKES A MISTAKE, IT'S NOT a big deal. There are other people around to help spot the error, or there are checks and balances built into the system so that errors are detected. And the mistake itself is generally not of the life-and-death variety, unless you are a fireman or a policeman. But there are numerous businesses in which an employee mistake will be attributed to "human error" in the newspapers, and it almost always gets traced back to inadequate training. Meanwhile, the interpretation by readers is that "human error" stands for poor work habits, a shoddy working environment in which errors abound, or conflicts within the company.

My friend Richard, like me, used to work for a commercial nuclear power plant. The guards at these facilities, unlike your typical security guards at department stores and chemical facilities, carry real guns that use real bullets. Because the United States government dictates security at a nuclear facility, guards are indeed trained to protect the property from any intruders. Once a guard at the Davis-Besse Nuclear Plant in Ohio accidentally shot his gun while cleaning it. The bullet passed through a couple of filing cabinets before it lodged in a wall. As the spokesperson for the facility, my friend Richard had to address the overwhelming media interest that resulted from the accidental shooting. "Human error" associated with any type of accident at a nuclear plant generally causes antinuclear activists to take note, and when they take action, the media generally follow up on their concerns. Richard had to escort several members of the media onto the property and show them the damage the gun caused. When a reporter asked why the guard had done it, Richard jokingly answered that the guard had told the filing cabinet to halt three times and it had not listened, so the guard shot it. Richard could get away with this humor because he knew all the reporters very well and had socialized with them, but he later confessed that he felt his joke would take the edge off of what was seen to be a rather embarrassing event for the facility. And he was right. For years after the incident, the plant was the center of both jokes and fear, as local residents came to realize that human error could occur at any type of organization. The bottom line is that you need to be prepared to discuss—and show through documentation—what type of training your employees have received.

What to Do

Provide as much training for your employees as possible so that "human error" does not come back to tarnish the reputation of your company. Also, ask your employees where they feel they need more training.

EMPLOYEE TRAINING TAKES UP TOO MUCH TIME

A HALLMARK OF SUCCESSFUL COMPANIES IS THAT THEY BREAK the mold; they are willing to do business in nontraditional ways. Being innovative helps them grow. The problem is that as they grow and take on new workers, more and more time must be spent in training employees about company routines and protocols.

What to Do

We've all read the success stories of entrepreneurs who brag about having done things their own way, with no business plan, no blueprint, no employee manual. They claim that instinct and "smarts" are what drove them and what made them successful. That may be true, but if you could look back in time into their operations, you would probably see a company with a lot of confused or anxious employees, a large turnover, and a seriously unstable growth period.

When employees join your company, they're going to bring with them what they learned in other businesses. Without a reference to turn to, they might proceed in a way that doesn't suit your company procedure, or they might demand the full-time attention of another employee.

The solution is to prepare a comprehensive operations manual. Such a reference will help to identify problems before they arise and will help solve them once they have been identified. A manual also offers the benefit of a training resource for new employees, a place they can go to get answers. If the manual is comprehensive, it will also provide the groundwork for objective decision making and fairness for treatment of employees.

Below is a list of suggested categories for developing an operations manual. Neither the categories nor the descriptions are complete; at all times, a manual should be tailored to the needs and practices of the company and its employees.

◆ **Introduction.** Include the company's history, philosophy, and guiding principles, and the purpose of the manual.

◆ **Organizational structure.** Include this in both chart and descriptive form. Identify the company's officers (by position, not person, so that it doesn't have to be updated as often), who reports to whom, and where all employees are located. It's also a good idea to put job descriptions here if possible.

◆ **Operating routines.** Offer instructions for routine tasks such as housekeeping duties, handling telephones, repairing equipment, controlling keys, getting cash advances and payment from expense forms, purchasing and stocking supplies, and interacting with visitors, customers, suppliers, regulatory agencies, consumer groups, inspectors, professional associations, etc. Also outline how different departments or groups within the company are to interact with one another.

◆ **Paper flow.** Provide samples of all forms and describe their use, outline when records are due and to whom, discuss billing routines and schedules for employee compensation, and give an explanation of the flow of paperwork that is expected.

◆ **Human resources.** Clearly state your hiring and firing policies. Provide examples of the employee forms you use. Describe employee benefits, vacations, holiday leave, hours, payroll deductions, frequency of salary reviews, and personal conduct you expect or abhor.

- **Products and services.** Describe your products and services and your target markets. Explain your customer service policy. Outline your procedures for sales and give an overview of the marketing/advertising efforts planned to carry them out.
- **Emergency procedures.** Even if you've developed a separate reference document for times of crisis (as described and recommended in Chapter 1), summarize your plans here. If you haven't prepared a separate manual, then be sure to cover everything here. You'll want to describe protection of the premises, personal security, handling of confidential information, how to deal with the news media, and how to handle fires, bomb threats, power failures, thefts, and accidents. Be sure to include emergency telephone numbers here, too.

Finally, put the manual in a binder so that it can be updated easily. Review it at least once a year, and if you can't give each employee a copy, place it in a common area so everyone has access to it without having to seek permission.

FIND BACKUP/TEMPORARY EMPLOYEES BEFORE YOU NEED THEM

THE SCENARIOS: IN THE MIDST OF FILLING A BIG ORDER AND requiring everyone to work overtime, you find that the entire staff comes down with the flu. A new competitor hires most of your staff away from you *all at the same time.* A carload of employees who carpool together are in an accident. A heavy snowfall, rainfall, or earthquake prevents employees from venturing to work (or they stay home with the kids because school has been canceled). The result is the same: you are left unexpectedly shorthanded to fulfill that big order. What do you do?

What to Do

The natural reaction is to take on more employees to handle the workload. It's important to stop at this point and think through the repercussions of acting too quickly: the order may be a one-time occurrence, and perhaps your paperwork is unfinished because you took time off last week. Consider taking on temporary employees for short-term, infrequent, unpredictable, and seasonal situations. Then, you'll be able to avoid these unexpected expenses and time wasters:

- the dollars required to advertise for, recruit, interview, and hire permanent employees
- the dollars lost to taxes, pensions, and severance
- being stuck with an employee who doesn't fit the corporate culture because you hired so hurriedly

Best of all, you'll be able to fulfill the order and finish the paperwork with few interruptions and no long-term repercussions. You also won't have to deal with the typical employee concerns: discussions about their professional futures, their benefits packages, their perceived need for more training and more challenges, or how their sick time and leave of absence options work.

Here's how to deal with the potential of a depleted staff. Make a list of former employees (if they left under good terms) and their phone numbers. Who better to call for help during an emergency than them? And while you're at it, talk to temporary agencies about your potential needs, fill out their paperwork, and become familiar with their procedures so that you can get employees on short notice.

YOU PRACTICE MORE "BUSYNESS" THAN BUSINESS

YOU HAVE LOTS OF EMPLOYEES. THEY'RE ALWAYS BUSY. IN FACT, they're tripping over one another in their haste to get things done and meet deadlines. They seem to be very efficient. Yet they are not very effective at achieving results, and your bottom line reflects it.

What to Do

True, this is not a potential crisis for which you need to activate a response team or call the news media, but it is a smoldering crisis all the same. You took on employees with certain expectations and results in mind, for which you were willing to exchange valued money (salary). As it turns out, your employees are taking the money but not delivering on the results.

First, you must accept that some clever employees can *appear* to be busy when they're not. Instead, they are busy trying to look busy.

For those employees who are truly busy, you need to recognize that efficiency does not necessarily result in effectiveness. Efficiency means producing with a minimum of waste, expense, and unnecessary effort. Effectiveness means producing *the right things* with a minimum of waste, expense, and unnecessary effort. Sure, they produce a high ratio of output to input, but if the output is not what you need, then their busyness will not result in business.

Some things you can do:

◆ **Observe your employees at work.** Are there too many interruptions? Are their meetings short and purposeful? Do they combine like tasks (such as running for office supplies) or do they double their own workload with unnecessary activities (such as picking up one item at a time as it runs out).

◆ **Reassess each person's talents and skills and what they actually like to do.** Recognize and respect differences in employee approaches to work. Trying to manage everyone on the staff in the same way will not work, because no two people carry out their jobs in the same way. Manage them as individuals, with awareness for their differences.

◆ **Determine whether employees understand the value of their work.** Do they consider their work worthwhile? What about the value of the work to the company? Employees do better work when they understand the answer to "What's in this for me?" The answer to this question must be clear. And I'm talking about more than money here; the value comes from realizing a sense of self-esteem from the work.

◆ **Review job descriptions.** Do they collectively reflect and fairly represent the total scope of work that must be done at your company, within the amount of time given to do it?

◆ **Consider whether employees are doing more, less, or about what their job descriptions say they will.**

◆ **Simplify your procedures for getting tasks done.** Perhaps there is too much redundancy or too many checks and balances.

◆ **Talk to your employees individually and collectively.** Let them identify obstacles to effectiveness.

◆ **Get rid of deadweight.** No company needs to keep poor performers who can't deliver results.

YOU'VE HIT A SLOW PERIOD BUT WANT TO KEEP EMPLOYEES

IF YOU'VE TAKEN THE TIME TO FIND THE BEST EMPLOYEES, then you'd be foolish to let them go when a temporary slow period hits.

What to Do

You have several options:

◆ Put them to work on improvement projects, research, or demographic studies. Think ahead to the time when your company is busy again. What will you wish you'd had them do when time was available?

◆ If the slow period is resulting in low cash, then ask them to work part-time and promise them a bonus when work picks up again, *if* you know you can deliver on that bonus.

◆ Also, ask your employees what they want to do. Some may want some time off for personal interests and will take it without pay if they know they will have jobs to come back to.

I know of an owner of a graphic arts studio and advertising firm near Cleveland who uses creativity to solve his slow periods. Rather than paying employees their full salaries during the two-to-three week slow period that occurs each year, he entered into an agreement with one of the printers he uses to "loan" his employees to them during that time. His employees are able to help the printer produce the overwhelming amount of yearbook printing jobs they get at that time every year, and the printer pays a percentage of their salaries. Everyone benefits from the arrangement: the printer is kept happy, the owner doesn't have to pay for down-time, and the employees say that the experience brings them up to speed on printing capabilities so that they can converse with clients more intelligently when they return to their regular work.

EMPLOYEES CAN COST YOU CUSTOMERS

TODAY'S LOYAL CUSTOMER CAN BE GONE TOMORROW—NEVER to be seen again. If your employees turn off even your best patrons with rude or inferior service, then you'll lose them to the competition. No matter what you have to offer, chances are there will be strong competition around to match it.

Don't be fooled into thinking that today's crowds will necessarily be there tomorrow. Just give them reason to turn away, and the competition will do all the rest. The result of poor customer service is no customers, and no customers equals no business. It's that simple. And in the case of independent bookstores and small hardware stores, even good customer service may not be enough to remain competitive with large superstores; instead, *exemplary* customer service is necessary, because it's the prime way that a small business can outdo its larger competition.

What to Do

Super customer service results in big sales because it is the best way to attract new business and to keep the old. Here's how to establish a first-rate customer service program that can translate into big profits over the years:

◆ **Devise formal company standards for dealing with customers.** Put your customer service policy in writing, and make sure that each employee complies. When Leslie Markle (not her real name), owner of a bookstore in Chicago, began getting complaints from customers about the rudeness of one of her employees, she made it a point to walk the floor more so that she could observe the employee's interactions with customers. "I never saw a problem. I couldn't understand what customers were talking about. Finally, I asked my aunt to come in one day when I was out, and I briefed her on how I expected customers to be treated. Sure enough, since I wasn't around, this employee treated my aunt with such disrespect and disinterest that I finally had enough reason to talk to her about her behavior. I don't know how many customers I lost before I finally addressed it with her. As a result, I now have formal written rules on how I expect customers to be treated. I even conduct role-play with employees when they're first hired." Markle now shares her experience with other small-business owners at local association meetings. "If business owners take the time to properly calculate the revenue lost to customers who left due to frustrations with poor service, the number they come up with would be so overwhelming, it would never again be an issue as to whether customer service quality is important to their business," Markle says.

◆ **Initiate a customer service suggestion program.** Place a suggestion box in the back room or stock area. Ask employees to drop in their ideas for improving the company's customer relations. To get them thinking, offer $25 for every idea the company puts into practice. This can produce some impressive results: employees are often in tune with what customers want. Additionally, employees get an appreciation for how serious you are about customer service.

◆ **Appoint a customer relations supervisor.** Choose an intelligent and levelheaded employee to supervise all customer relations on a daily basis. In small companies this need not be the individual's only assignment, but there should be one person with the authority and the knowledge to handle customers.

DISCRIMINATION STILL EXISTS

DESPITE SOCIETY'S AWARENESS OF DISCRIMINATION AND THE legal ramifications that accompany it, many small businesses still suffer from it. If you suspect that any employee is not treating someone fairly, you will need to step in and take action to protect your employees and yourself.

What to Do

Determine what is causing the perceived discrimination. One way to do this is to observe employees outside of the office at company functions such as sporting events or picnics. In this situation, you may find an employee is being rejected due to irritating behavior that occurs only in the office, rather than as a result of prejudices against race, sex, or religion. If this is the situation, talk to the employees to find out what their grievances are. A business owner once shared a story with me about a minority employee who felt shunned by the rest of the staff. In a panic, the owner launched an investigation into why this person was being treated as he was. As it turned out, the employee had a hygiene problem that offended the other workers. Had he not pressed for answers, the owner could have ended up with a discrimination suit against his company.

If an allegation has been made against an employee, talk

to the person making the accusations. Then talk to any witnesses. Document your conversations in writing. Show employees that you are making an effort to resolve the situation in as fair a manner as possible. If you feel the accusation is unfair, talk to the person who filed the complaint and explain why you feel this way, but never deny him or her the chance to file the complaint. If you believe the accusation is true, then take corrective action. Sometimes training may suffice. Other times you may have to fire the offender. Make sure all your employees are familiar with your company's policy regarding discrimination.

SEXUAL HARASSMENT IS A CONCERN IN ANY COMPANY

SEXUAL HARASSMENT IS NOT JUST A CONCERN FOR BIG BUSInesses; small businesses can experience the fines, legalities, and decreased morale that accompany harassment, too. In 1997, a woman in California was awarded a whopping $6.6 million for having been subjected to sexual comments from her coworkers at a small business, a car dealership. And the American Psychological Association reports that of all working women in organizations of all sizes, 40 to 60 percent have reported being subjected to sexual harassment of some type.

Further, the Civil Rights Act of 1991 says that a company with fewer than 100 workers can be made to pay up to $50,000 in damages as a result of a sexual harassment case in which the company has been found to be negligent.

All this means that sexual harassment is not something to be taken lightly. However, according to statistics from the Institute for Crisis Management in Louisville, Kentucky, sexual harassment went up 390 percent from 1990 to 2000. Approximately 15,500 cases were filed in 1998 alone, compared to 6,900 in 1991.

 What to Do

Sexual harassment is serious and costly business; that's why every business—no matter how small—should have a written policy in place. According to federal regulations, a business is responsible for sexual harassment in the workplace "where the employer knows or should have known of the conduct."

Rather than ignoring the topic, prepare yourself now so that you have legal defense if sexual harassment occurs in your company:

◆ Write and distribute a clear policy prohibiting sexual harassment of any kind at your company. Have employees acknowledge in writing that they have read and understand the ramifications of violating it. Under federal law, you—as employer—are automatically liable for an employee's behavior at work unless you can show that you wrote and distributed a policy prohibiting sexual harassment.

◆ Take seriously any reports of sexual harassment. Document all complaints in writing and include as many details as possible.

◆ Talk to witnesses of the alleged event and record their comments, too.

◆ Talk to your attorney if the employee threatens to file a complaint.

COMPANY INFORMATION IS IN JEOPARDY DUE TO A RESIGNING EMPLOYEE

DESPITE YOUR BEST HIRING PRACTICES, EMPLOYEE BENEFITS, and compensation packages, employees will leave you from time to time. The reasons will be many: a better opportunity elsewhere, to try something new, to find more/better benefits, to go back to school, a move to a new location, to stay home with family, to start their own business, etc. Before you panic, however, remember that you may have options.

What to Do

When a key employee wants to leave, don't react in anger. Instead, consider sweetening his or her deal to keep this valued employee in the company. In the disappointment of the moment, it's easy to overlook this option, but it could be your best bet. And your offer doesn't have to involve pay. Remember, the benefits an employee receives from work go far beyond the actual amount you pay in wages. Sometimes, benefits other than compensation are what an employee has wanted: new title, better hours, more health care options, better working conditions, more/less responsibility, or more help, to name a few.

Talk to the employee. You may find that something has been annoying the employee about his or her coworkers or the work environment that has never been mentioned. Perhaps the person assumed that you knew but were doing nothing about it.

Several of the best defenses for your company when an employee leaves actually should take place long before the resignation has a chance to occur.

◆ **Job descriptions are an excellent tool to discourage resignation.** Although the law doesn't require job descriptions, they can be used as a tool to evaluate candidates, and a tool candidates can use to evaluate a job before hiring on, rather than deciding to "try it and if I don't like it, I'll just quit." A job description provides prospective employees with an idea of the duties involved in the job they're applying for—ensuring you both have the same view of their job responsibilities while providing a means for evaluating performance and a little more security that the employee is doing a job that he or she wants to do. Besides—and this is to your benefit—job descriptions make it much easier to fire an employee for poor performance, because you've established written guidelines in advance.

◆ **A second defensive measure to take before risking the loss of a well-informed employee is to limit access to inside information in the first place.** Essentially, departing employees can take two things with them: relationships and information. If you maintain a primary or overriding connection with customers, departing employees will find it tough to build relationships that they can later work to their advantage. Regardless of whether specific knowledge is legally protectable as a trade secret, employees can't steal what they don't know about. Of course, this leaves you being virtually a continued one-person show since you don't share your knowledge or decision-making authority with any employees. Good employees will begin to get frustrated, even angry, if they are not made to feel that they are trusted and are in on things. That's why your best option may be to inform your employees of the company's knowledge but to protect that knowledge in another way, as the following option describes.

◆ **Your third and probably best defense is legal documentation in the form of contracts and noncompete agreements.** As long as employees are on the company payroll, they are legally expected to remain loyal to their employers. Therefore, a contract can specify that employees planning their departure can't solicit the company's customers, talk coworkers into leaving with them, promote their new company, or neglect their jobs. (However, they can prepare for their departure by preparing a business plan, forming or buying a company, and, in certain cases, telling current customers they're leaving to start a new business.)

Noncompete agreements prohibit departing employees from competing in the same business as their ex-employer in a defined geographical area for a specified period of time. Be aware, however, that covenants not to compete are one of the most litigated areas in employment law. They're valid in most states if the restrictions are *reasonable* in scope and duration. The key word is reasonable. Generally, the law allows these restrictions if they're narrowly drawn and designed to protect the employer, not just to stop competition. If challenged, an aggressive company that has imposed an overly broad restriction may have to answer for it in court—and the court may strike the entire agreement rather than whittle it down to size.

Unfortunately, there are no firm rules for how long you can restrict a former employee from competing with you. It varies from case to case, depending on such factors as how long it would take your company to replace the employee and how often the departing employee was in contact with customers.

An exiting employee could also sabotage equipment or computers or compromise trade secrets—formulas, recipes, patterns, devices, or compilations of information you use in your company that give you a competitive advantage. Information as routine—and seemingly innocuous—as a customer list or fee scale, or as complex as an invention or software program, may constitute a trade secret. To determine proprietary property, courts consider whether anyone outside your company knows the information, which people in your company know it, what measures were taken to maintain secrecy, the value of the information, and how easily it could be legally acquired or duplicated.

Ann King, one of two owners of Atlanta-based Blooming Cookies Catalog, learned the hard way to protect vital company information. By entrepreneurial standards, she got off to a great start when founding Blooming. The business was growing, but she couldn't afford to purchase her own commercial oven, so she contracted with a small bakery in Smyrna, Georgia. "I didn't have it in writing at the time that my recipe was proprietary information, so someone at the bakery shared it with another company they were working with. And that company went on to become very well known for the recipe."

Although the law requires employees to stay mum about their employer's trade secrets, a company may have confidential information that doesn't qualify for this protection. Thus having new employees sign a nondisclosure or confidentiality agreement protecting all sensitive information is smart business. Such an agreement can identify the information to be protected, impress upon the employee the seriousness of the obligation, and provide critical evidence if there's ever a dispute.

Talk to your attorney about adding a liquidated damages clause. It establishes the amount of money departing employees must pay you if they take your customers while a noncompete or nonsolicitation restriction is in force. Similarly, you can penalize departing employees by having them forfeit specific postemployment benefits if they breach their nondisclosure or noncompete agreements. Work with your attorney now to safeguard your company from departing employees in the future.

For more on employees and computer sabotage, see Chapter 5.

PLAN FOR EXECUTIVE SUCCESSION AND CONTINUITY

MANY SMALL BUSINESSES HAVE FOLDED——ESPECIALLY FAMILY-owned businesses—because no one was trained to take over in case of unexpected leave or death. We've all heard the stories of how too many executives were flying in a plane that crashed. Sometimes an entrepreneur suddenly finds himself without decision makers and people "in the know" due to a host of personal situations.

As Allen Fields learned, "People change, and sometimes they change in surprising ways in a short period of time." Fields, who owned a computer training company near New Orleans, lost his two top leaders at the same time. "One day my CEO was king of business for me. I had no worries. The company was doing well. The next thing I know, he had left town to run off with my president. He left a wife, three kids, and my company behind. Suddenly, nobody was left to run the company, because my three vice presidents were all fighting over the available positions and trying to figure out how to continue operations. I didn't even have anybody left that knew the highest-level responsibilities. I learned the hard way to ensure that other employees were groomed and kept informed of vital company information." Fields has since sold the company and left the world of entrepreneurship.

What to Do

If you're one of the many entrepreneurs who have hired a CEO or president to oversee your company, make sure that someone is being groomed to assume the position in case you lose your top employee.

FAMILIES OF EMPLOYEES NEED ATTENTION, TOO

WHEN YOU ADD TO YOUR WORKFORCE, YOU DON'T JUST HIRE an employee; you also hire an employee's family. Your employee will talk about, complain about, and boast about work at home. Family members will get impressions of your company that they will share with friends and relatives who may just happen to be customers or prospects. If the family is not happy with the company, you may have a problem, because family members don't feel the same inhibitions about bad-mouthing the company that the employee does.

What to Do

There are many ways companies use to build good relationships with employees' families, from company picnics to newsletters discussing family safety that are mailed to the home. But this book is not about developing relationships; it's about preserving them so that the company can survive. Thus, my advice is to communicate with families too when you experience an unexpected turn of events. This can be done as easily as providing an explanation to employees in writing and encouraging them to share it with their families. A cautionary note, however: Just because something is intended for the eyes of employees and families only doesn't mean that other people won't see it. Keep that in mind every time you put something in writing.

Communicating with employees' families may mean that you will have to talk with them right at your place of work. I have seen several situations in which an employee got hurt at work and, because off-site assistance was called, word went out to the public that someone at the XYZ Corporation had been hurt. In such instances, family members immediately begin calling the offices, and if they can't get through, go to the office. This means in an emergency you might need a place designated for families that is away from negative discussions and, especially, the news media. Determine that location now, and let key supervisors know what area you have chosen.

WHEN YOU HAVE TO FIRE AN EMPLOYEE

SUPPOSE YOU'VE GOT AN EMPLOYEE WHO BREAKS EVERY RULE in the book—you name it. He's always late for work. He cheats on expense forms. He bad-mouths the company. He makes passes at female coworkers. He hasn't met one agreed-upon performance objective in the past six months. In frustration, you fire him at the end of the day Monday. Come Tuesday, your bad experience turns into a nightmare when you learn that your ex-employee is suing you.

What to Do

Do your homework before you fire someone. To legally establish just cause for firing an employee, you must prove serious incompetence, misconduct, or disregard for company policies and give the employee sufficient opportunity to correct his or her problems. If you've done that but the employee remains a problem, then you may have reason to terminate employment. Always check with your legal counsel first to avoid a wrongful-dismissal suit.

Never make light of a dismissal. Remember that the person you're letting go has worked side-by-side with your other employees and perhaps your suppliers, customers, and even competitors. Chances are, the person you want to fire has made friends and confidants of some of these people. Handle the situation carefully, and show respect for the person you're thinking about letting go. Let him or her maintain dignity. The last thing you want to do is damage your reputation with these onlookers. In general, follow these guidelines:

◆ Let all your employees know what you expect of them before a misunderstanding or negative situation can occur.

◆ Provide them with their own copies of company policies and practices.

◆ Create a system by which you and your employees can identify when things are not going as you plan, so that they have a chance to change. An annual or six-month performance appraisal can help.

◆ Talk to the employee who is causing problems and give him a chance to voice his side of the story. Perhaps he simply doesn't have the right tools to get his job done. Perhaps his working conditions aren't sufficient for a personal handicap, such as poor eyesight.

◆ Document all your actions carefully. Be very specific in your notes, recording all conversations, details, and dates. Make sure the employee is aware of what you write and place in his or her personnel file.

◆ Fire the employee if necessary, if you've given him ample opportunity and time to change.

When it comes time to fire the person, ask yourself: if an

employee is fired in private, will anybody hear it? No, and that's the point. Terminating employment should be done away from coworkers, even if you have to take the employee out of the office to do so. Do it after hours or before hours if necessary. Directors of personnel programs will tell you that Friday is the best day to fire somebody; it gives the employee the weekend to cool off and restore some dignity.

Do not take fired personnel back to their desk or locker in front of their coworkers. It's too embarrassing for both the terminated employee and those still employed. If you have to, mail them their personal belongings the next day.

Another reason not to allow a dismissed employee to return to his or her place of work after being fired is to protect yourself, your employees, and your business. Disgruntled employees may want to exact a pound of flesh by misfiling critical information, shredding vital papers, causing computer malfunctions, crippling machinery, starting a fire, misplacing critical tools or fixtures, marring furniture and walls, hurting someone, or stealing from the company. Another step to secure yourself is to keep records of past employees to aid police in future investigations.

◆ Schedule an exit interview in which you talk about the reason for the termination and make the employee aware of any privileges that exist upon termination, such as severance pay or unemployment benefits.

◆ Have a third person join in on the exit interview so that you have a witness as to what was discussed.

To maintain good relations, cut down on the potential of a lawsuit, and demonstrate compassion to other employees, don't let terminated employees leave empty-handed. Give them some severance pay, or offer to pay for some community college classes or for a few months at a job placement program. You want to make sure you're not just throwing them out on the street for the peace of mind of everyone involved: you, the employee, and the coworkers who witness the whole process. Make it look like you're trying to help them get their future going again.

The basic reason for handling terminations with diplomacy? Every year, thousands of unhappily terminated employees sue their former employers. Their complaints, justified or not, cost small-business owners millions of dollars in legal fees and lost time and productivity.

HIRING IN HASTE IS RISKY BUSINESS

IT'S TIME TO HIRE A NEW EMPLOYEE; YOUR GOALS ARE TO DO it quickly and inexpensively because, in your mind, recruiting time is unproductive time. However, this is precisely when you need to slow down and take the time to hire the right person.

Hiring an employee is always full of risk, but what if you unwittingly hire a drunk driver, child molester, or convicted felon? Your company could be in serious jeopardy if someone seeks to sue the culprit's employer—you.

What to Do

Of course you have to hire the person who feels right to you, for the job and for the tasks that need to be accomplished. Many factors go into hiring the right person, and other authors have written entire books about how to do a thorough search for the right employee. In this one, I'm simply going to summarize four bits—albeit vital bits—of advice related to guarding yourself during hiring:

◆ **Expect to pay for expertise.** If you want to pay someone minimum wage yet expect the quality of a salaried employee, remember the old saying "You get what you pay for." Be willing to pay what the "right" person is worth so that the "wrong" person won't make your company vulnerable thanks to his errors and mistakes, or use more of your vital time for training than necessary.

◆ **Do a thorough background check.** Insist on references, and check them all. Call previous employers, colleges, and personal references to make sure the applicant has actually held the positions and earned the degrees claimed.

◆ **Get your questions ready.** Be sure you know what types of questions you can't ask, including questions about age, ethnicity, religious affiliation, and marital or family status. If you're concerned about how an applicant's personal life might affect work performance, then ask questions that are designed to reveal the answer but are focused on the job. Instead of asking whether an applicant is willing to be away from his or her family for periods of time, for example, ask whether or not the applicant is willing to travel. Instead of asking whether the employee might miss work when children are home from school during snow days or illnesses, ask whether the applicant is comfortable with the advertised hours or whether flextime might be needed.

◆ **Put new hires on a probation period.** This makes it easier for you to let them go than if they thought they had permanency at your company.

ESTABLISH SECURITY IF YOUR BUSINESS IS IN YOUR HOME

WHEN YOU BRING EMPLOYEES INTO YOUR HOME, YOUR WHOLE life may be revealed to them, from how you treat your kids to where you shop to what foods you eat. Worse yet, your employees will become intimately familiar with your family's home routines and your possessions.

Joyce Nylor, a freelance chemical engineer, brought a nanny into her home to watch her young son while she worked. "I had to leave my home for occasional meetings, which meant that the nanny was alone with my son in the house," Nylor says. "That was a mistake. You see, clothes are my passion. I even converted an extra bedroom into a closet to store all my suits and outfits. One day, I couldn't find a suit I was sure was back from the cleaner. Then about a week later, I couldn't find two other ones. As time went by, different outfits kept disappearing. Finally, one day I was driving by a local secondhand clothing store and a little voice told me to stop in and look around. I found seven of my suits hanging on the racks, waiting to be sold. My nanny had been selling them to the shop."

Nylor isn't alone in her frustration with bringing an employee into the home. David Wilson (not his real name), who runs a graphic design business from his Wilmington, Delaware, home, hired a local college student to assist him part-time. Because the girl was an art major, he thought he was doing her a double favor by letting her gain income and experience. Imagine his surprise when his home was robbed with no signs of visible entry, and it turned out to be his employee's boyfriend. "I found out afterward that he had borrowed her keys once and had made a copy of a key to my house. Of course I had let her have free reign of the place so that she could use the bathroom and get food from the refrigerator, so she had shared with her boyfriend the details of the possessions in my house. In the end, I had to let her go, too, even though I believed her to be innocent; there were just too many bad feelings left over for us to be able to work together."

🐾 What to Do

Establish limits for an employee's use of and access to your home. Review them during the interview process, and see if the potential employee can work under your conditions. Try to limit the amount of time that you are away from home when your employee is there working. If you have to be away often, stop in unexpectedly, but don't explain why you've changed your routine. See more ideas under "Know Whom You Can Trust," on page 139.

Also bear in mind that if you work out of your home, a special zoning permit may be required for you to take on employees. You may also need additional insurance; make sure you've got liability coverage in case an employee is injured on your property.

WHEN AN EMPLOYEE GETS INJURED

DESPITE YOUR BEST SAFETY PRACTICES, EMPLOYEES CAN GET hurt. Even a basic office can have stairs to fall down, garbage cans to trip over, spilled water by the water fountain to slip on, filing drawers that fall on feet, and letter openers that can puncture skin.

🐾 What to Do

Limit both your number of injured employees and the resulting lawsuits by doing the following:

◆ Make sure help can be called easily. Are phones accessible? Easy to use? Are emergency numbers posted? Can an ambulance easily reach you from the road?

- Keep a first-aid kit handy. Ensure that employees know its location.

- Establish a policy whereby a supervisor accompanies an injured person to the hospital. The supervisor can keep you updated back at the office on the employee's condition, warn you of any news media that might be arriving at the hospital, and keep the injured person from feeling abandoned by the company.

- Find out how you would learn which hospital an injured employee has been taken to if another employee doesn't ride along. Just because an ambulance leaves for the County West Hospital doesn't mean it won't end up at the County East if it finds out on the way that County West can't handle the emergency. Check with the local dispatch to find out where the ambulance delivered your employee.

CAN YOU HANDLE AN EMPLOYEE DEATH?

IF YOUR CEO (OR OTHER KEY EXECUTIVE OR EMPLOYEE) IS injured or killed during nonworking hours, does his or her spouse and family know the people at your organization to call so that an appropriate response can be delivered before word goes public? Whereas a large corporation may have to worry about stock taking a nosedive under such conditions, a small organization may have to worry about vendors', suppliers', and customers' impressions of the company's viability. Both situations could be disastrous for a company's bottom line. Likewise, what if an employee dies at work? Do you have phone numbers ready and counseling lined up for the other employees?

What to Do

Have phone numbers of employees' families readily available, and be sure that your employees' families know how to get in touch with key personnel at the office. Develop procedures to ensure that the family finds out about deaths or injuries from either you or another designated employee rather than from a stranger who works at the hospital. Your compassion during such stressful times will be noted by the other employees.

EMPLOYEES WILL TALK DURING AN EMERGENCY

SADLY, IF YOU WANT NEGATIVE INFORMATION TO GET OUT quickly, tell it to an employee during a crisis. I have seen employees contact relatives, friends, neighbors, and even the local news media (for the $50 reward for the hot news tip of the day) during emergencies. This means that—if left on their own—employees can make you very vulnerable to bad publicity, rumors, and misunderstandings during an adverse situation.

According to Institute for Crisis Management research, about 9 percent of all business crisis stories that appear in the print media—regardless of the size of the business—cite employees as sources of information. Other sources include judicial representatives (police, officers of the court, judges), just over 28 percent; governmental representatives (elected and regulatory), about 29 percent; customers and consumers, 12 percent; union leaders, 10 percent; business owners and executives, 7 percent; and activists, about 5 percent.

 What to Do

Take the time today—before any emergencies are in sight— to call your employees together to discuss how you want emergencies handled. Chapter 7 offers more advice on how to brief employees to talk to (or *not* to talk to) the news media and other outsiders. Make employees aware that you have a procedure prepared for crisis times, and let them know how it functions. Tell them who is on the response team (see Chapter 1), and explain that even though they don't have an official role during crisis times, they will be involved in the response by continuing operations as best they can and by not discussing the situation with anyone. In return, promise them that you'll keep them informed by giving them updates on the crisis. And when the time comes that you actually do experience a crisis, what should you tell your employees? The truth to the following questions:

◆ What is the company's position?

◆ How stable are their jobs?

◆ Should they report to (or stay at) work?

◆ Should they report to work tomorrow?

- Will they be paid?
- How will they be kept informed/told what to do?
- Should they/can they call their families?
- How did this situation happen?
- What will be changed to make sure it doesn't happen again?

RUMORS CAN TARNISH YOUR COMPANY'S GOOD NAME

WHEN IT COMES TO RUMORS, PERCEPTION IS REALITY. IT doesn't matter what the truth is; if your employees, customers, or neighbors have a different impression of your organization, then that is the reality with which you must deal.

Riverboat Bed and Breakfast experienced a drastic drop in bookings after the company made the local paper due to rumors of a bomb onboard. Owners Joe and Dixie Bolduc (not their real names) operate their 123-foot-long, three-deck stern-wheeler in Oregon, hosting guests for overnight trips on the river. "One of our boilers blew," Joe says. "We followed our emergency procedures closely. Unfortunately, part of these procedures included having instructed employees not to talk to passengers about the problem. Before long, the passengers were sharing the rumor that a bomb had gone off and that a second one was hidden onboard somewhere. Everyone panicked. Most of the passengers asked to be let off the boat. They, of course, began to talk to everyone about their experience. It ended up in the local paper. The whole thing was a nightmare. When we powwowed about it later with the employees, several of them volunteered that they had heard passengers spreading the rumor about a bomb. When I asked why they hadn't told the passengers what had really happened, they reminded me of their instructions to not talk about adverse situations with the passengers. You can bet I changed that practice quickly. Now rumors are brought to my attention immediately."

What to Do

When rumors run rampant, make it easy for your employees to report them to you. Periodically let them know that you want them to come to you with concerns about what people are saying and thinking about the business.

When a rumor has caused your company harm, circle the wagons. Call employees in and regroup by discussing the rumor, telling them the truth, and supplying them with correct information they then can share with everyone outside your doors.

The effectiveness of your internal communications can have an immense impact in building trust and goodwill with employees, as well as lessen your chances of being blindsided by reporters who have picked up information from someone on the inside. In addition to the grapevine, how do your management and employees find out what is going on? How can you ensure that those people and the families of the participants get the word on any major disclosure from you and not from the news media? Here are the tactics you should adopt:

◆ Have a checklist of key people to be contacted, and designate one of your best people to make sure the participants, your management and employees, and especially family members are not caught by surprise when a disclosure is made. If something newsworthy comes up during a briefing, that person should be responsible for alerting any participants it relates to. In some instances they may have to draft a statement summarizing the question, the response, and any clarification that might be needed. The statement can then be used to update employees and for response to subsequent media inquiries.

◆ Distribute employee bulletins so you can get updates posted in a hurry.

◆ Provide employees with a daily compilation of prominent news clips and a summary of your conversations with reporters so they will know what the media are reporting about the situation and the company.

◆ Establish a system for providing all of your locations (anywhere you have employees) with relevant information on the news events and any important developments disclosed to the news media.

Your employees will appreciate your efforts to keep them informed. Those at the location where the story is breaking also will appreciate suggestions on how to respond to questions from reporters when an encounter occurs. Most employees are leery of being interviewed, but they also don't want to be discourteous, fearing that the reporter will use their negative response to make them or their organization look bad. So help them out by scheduling orientation sessions regarding the impending news story and giving your employees some guidance in how to handle an impromptu interview. Encourage them to contact you if they are approached by a member of the press and asked specific questions.

For more on how to handle rumors and accusations about your company, see Chapter 7.

KNOW WHOM YOU CAN TRUST

OF COURSE, THE BEST RULE OF THUMB IS TO SURROUND YOURself with the best staff you can find and one that you trust. However, people change, circumstances change, and people change in reaction to circumstances. Often these circumstances may be beyond your control. You will experience a lot of extra stress if you have a staff you don't trust, regardless of whether that trust applies to thievery, simple nosiness, gossip, or outright rudeness to customers. But I've talked with many small-business owners who experienced more than stress after finding out the hard way that they had an employee they should not have trusted; in one instance of sabotaged computer equipment and destroyed files, the owner had no option but to close doors and begin his career again as an employee for someone else.

What to Do

If you have a staff—or even just one employee—that you distrust, you're going to have to establish ways to protect yourself and your business:

♦ **Announce your location.** Whenever you leave work for any reason, give your staff clear information on your destination, length of absence, and how you can be reached. Instruct the staff to contact you immediately concerning any important business development; be sure to define "important" for them. Make it clear that no one is to make decisions for you.

◆ **Identify who is in charge.** Assign one key employee to serve as manager in your absence. Inform all employees of this assignment, and direct them to come to this individual when you are not available.

◆ **Be available.** Don't leave your business on a regular basis or for extended periods of time. If extensive work on the road is required, try to delegate the work to an employee. There is simply no substitute for the owner-manager running things at the main location of business. Just the presence of authority is usually sufficient to discourage most excesses.

◆ **Run periodic checks on the company.** The best way to determine how your employees are performing is to check on their work—and their honesty—without prior notice. One good technique is to have someone else call the company in the guise of a potential customer. See what kind of service they get. Or ask a friend to visit your place of business and make a purchase. Have the person check to see that all purchases are properly rung up. A simple check like this can save many thousands of dollars and will help to ease your concerns.

◆ **Conduct audits regularly.** Have your accountant audit all the books on a regular basis, reviewing all possible areas of employee fraud.

◆ **Implement security measures.** Keep private things available only to yourself, or in a centralized location that can be supervised. Have follow-up checking procedures so you know where critical documents and data are at all times. If your company is small enough, keeping all sensitive material in one supervised, locked file cabinet may be a solution.

Legal Concerns

ONE MISTAKE MADE BY BUSINESS OWNERS IS HAVING INCOM-plete personnel policies and procedures. Personnel programs are not left to the sole discretion of business owners in our modern business world. Even well-meaning policies that previously proved successful may conflict with the legal regulations that all employers must abide by today.

GOT EMPLOYEES? THEN YOU'VE GOT LEGAL OBLIGATIONS

CHIEF AMONG THE GOVERNMENT REGULATIONS FOR EMPLOYERS today are minimum wage laws, fair employment regulations, the right of employees to collective bargaining and to form their own unions, requirements for withholding income taxes and other items from employee paychecks for the federal government, and equal employment opportunity provisions.

What to Do

Periodically check the current status of all personnel regulations. Failure to comply could lead to disastrous unexpected consequences. Employers are expected to keep up with all the changes and new requirements. You can get in trouble if it can be proved there's been a lack of attention to employment-related issues. Unfortunately, not knowing labor law is no defense when an employer gets sued by an angry employee. Also, be sure to document problems as they occur. It's much better to take a half hour and document employee problems now so that you can better defend yourself in court later.

Fringe benefits, health and safety programs, profit-sharing plans, pensions, and vacation policies are all part of a complete personnel program today. Successful business owners must recognize that fair and competitive wages, attractive fringe benefits, desirable working conditions, and a sense of concern for employees are important parts of building a staff of dedicated employees. And dedicated employees are who you want on staff to cut down on employee-caused crises and to stand by you when the unexpected occurs.

VIRTUAL EMPLOYEES CHANGE THE RULES LEGALLY

IF YOUR COMPANY IS LOCATED IN YOUR HOME OR A CRAMPED office, then you may be considering hiring a virtual employee. Like other aspects of employee relations, the pros and cons of hiring a virtual employee are best left to a book dedicated to human resources and employee protocols. What I'm concerned about in this book is that you protect yourself when taking on a virtual employee.

What to Do

One advantage of hiring virtual employees is the ability to hire anywhere in the country—or the world; however, this means that your employee will subject you to some new hiring routines. For example, before hiring an out-of-state employee, be sure to check the legal and tax requirements of the state (or country) in which that employee works and resides. You will probably be required to establish a tax filing status as employer in each state in which you have an employee, because each state has its own regulations regarding state tax, unemployment contributions, and workers' compensation and disability insurance, among other things.

Hiring requirements vary from state to state. Even states that don't have a state income tax require you to file payroll deductions for other employment benefits. The good news is that you may not have to file as an employer in your own state if you have no employees in that state. To find out the regulations and filing requirements in the state in which your employee resides, contact that state's department of licensing or its employment services bureau.

Other requirements apply regardless of what state you (or your employees) reside in:

◆ To register as an employer, you must obtain a Federal Employer Identification Number. You can obtain this by filing IRS Form SS-4. You also need to obtain and keep on file an Employee's Withholding Certificate (W-4) and Employment Eligibility Verification form (Form I-9) for each of your employees.

◆ You are required to report new hires to the state agency responsible for child support issues, generally within twenty days. If you have employees in more than one state, you can make a single report to the national Office of Child Support Enforcement at 202-401-9267 or www.acf.dhhs.gov/programs/cse/newhire/nh/nh.htm.

◆ If your employee works in another state, you may be responsible for payroll reporting and taxes only to that state. If, however, your employee works in your state part of the time, you may be responsible for reporting payroll taxes to both states. Check with your state employment office for details.

◆ If your employee generates revenue for your company in another state (e.g., by selling your products or taking on clients in that state), you have to apply for a business license in that state and pay any appropriate fees and sales and use taxes. For information on taxes, employee benefits, and hiring regulations, see the U.S. Department of Labor Small Business Handbook at www.dol.gov/dol/asp/public/programs/handbook/contents.htm.

The Bottom Line

CREATING GOOD EMPLOYEE RELATIONS ISN'T JUST A NICE thing to do—in the end, it directly affects your bottom line. Taking a proactive approach to management is crucial to creating a positive environment that will foster harmony for both owner and employee.

CHAPTER 5

Ease Your Vulnerability to Computer Problems

ITH THE GROWTH OF
e-commerce has come the growth of cyber head-
aches and headlines: "Melissa Virus Costs Millions";
"DDoS Wipes Out Yahoo! And Others"; "Republican
Web Site Defaced with Pro-Gore Messages";
"Bubbleboy Virus Introduces New Concern"; "Los
Alamos Loses Top-Secret Hard Drive"; "LoveLetter
Damage Estimated at Whopping $10 Billion"; and
"Credit Card Vitals Stolen at CDUniverse."

Although disparity may exist between large and
small businesses in many respects, this sadly is not
the case when it comes to high-tech problems. All
companies, regardless of size, can get caught in the
cyber catch-22, wherein it's impossible to build a
company without computer equipment and a Web
presence, but it's next to impossible to protect yourself and your company once you buy that equipment
and establish a Web presence.

What can happen? You could be the victim of hardware breakdowns or corrupted software, or the target of competitive snoops, hackers, customers with fraudulent credit cards, disgruntled employees, vandals, or a host of anonymous computer-savvy thieves who make a living at lifting or altering things on the Internet. A survey published in *Information Week* magazine, and conducted by PricewaterhouseCoopers, estimates that companies of all sizes lost a combined $1.6 trillion in revenue in 1999 due to downtime resulting from computer security breaches, vandals, and virus attacks. In another survey, the Gartner Group reports a 12-to-1 ratio for the number of times online merchants suffered credit card fraud compared to their offline, brick-and-mortar counterparts.

Besides countless hours you'll have to spend in reproducing data, replacing equipment, recovering from lost revenue, or restoring your reputation, you may find yourself unwittingly in trouble legally for breaches of privacy, plagiarism, slander, or failure to fulfill a contract.

To make matters worse, employees and other insiders continue to pose a more serious security threat than outsiders, according to Andy Briney, editor of *Information Security* magazine (www.infosecuritymag.com). The magazine's 2000 Information Security Industry Survey found that "companies experiencing an electronic theft, sabotage, or disclosure of proprietary information grew by 41 percent in the last year [from 1999]," Briney says. Although this survey is geared toward large businesses, the numbers speak to the growing concern of inside security threats for businesses of all sizes.

Given the benefits the standard office computer brings to a business, it's hard to imagine how vulnerable it makes that same business. Even exposure to viruses and strategic mistakes in e-mail use can wreak havoc in an office. After all, every word of every message employees send out is stored, archived, and backed up, making it accessible by hackers and competitors and potentially opening the business owner up to defamation, discrimination, and exposure of company secrets or marketing information.

The physical safety of your computers is worth thinking about also. Even in a home office, a computer can be damaged by heat, smoke, magnetic effects, vibration and shock, static electricity, and electrical storms.

When it comes to computers, *Success* magazine (May 1999) says most small-business owners share "the same, fundamental nightmares, the four most common being about (1) vendors who refuse to service the equipment they sell, (2) systems crashes, (3) security breaches that threaten the lifeblood of the business, and (4) the sudden departure of an internal tech guru or IT manager. Each of these four situations can in reality bring a business to a screeching halt. And traditionally, each of them requires a very expensive response, which is exactly why small, usually cash-strapped, businesses have such a hard time obtaining assistance."

This chapter will simplify the preventive steps you can take now to avoid these and other troubles. Of course you'll have to pick and choose from the advice; what is pertinent to a home-based business sporting one computer may be of little concern to an office of 100 people dealing with a local area network.

Preventive Steps

BACKUPS ARE A MUST—NOT A MAYBE

I HAVE TALKED WITH MORE THAN ONE FRUSTRATED BUSINESS owner who, when a computer problem hit, realized too late that all the vital information he needed to recover from the problem was stored—you guessed it—on the computer that crashed.

 What to Do

Don't make this same mistake. As soon as possible, type and print out key computer and hardware data, such as setup information, tech support numbers, serial numbers and product identification numbers, software supplier numbers, e-mail passwords, and ISP (Internet Service Provider) account settings.

149

We all know we're supposed to keep backups of all data, and in a different location than our PC so that they aren't destroyed together. But when Dorsey Trailers in Elba, Alabama, was hit by a flood, their backup records and files didn't do them much good. "They were stored in a bank vault, but the bank was flooded, too," says Marilyn Marks, CEO of this manufacturing firm that makes tractor trailer truck beds. Marks recommends keeping vital documents and backup computer files at least fifty miles away.

Here's a backup shortcut to use on a tightly scheduled day: if you're racing to get out the door and just can't take the time to make a full backup copy to protect that project you've worked on all day, then simply e-mail a copy to yourself. That way, if your computer is tampered with before your return, you'll still be able to retrieve the information by logging onto your account from another computer. Better still, use a free e-mail service such as Excite Mail (www.excite.com) or Yahoo! Mail (www.yahoo.com). This way you can retrieve your mail from any PC that has an Internet connection.

For backing up information regularly, you have choices: do it yourself using a local tape drive or hard disk, store all files simultaneously on a mirror drive, or do it online. If you do it yourself, consider backing up not only data but applications, too. Although data backups are faster and easier, you'll have to reinstall your applications from the original CD-ROMs if you experience a crash. You have several choices for backup, from OnStream's Internal IDE, which holds as much as 30GB of data on a single tape, to Iomega's Zip drive, which can hold several hundred megabytes of information. If you choose to store backups online, you can look into services—such as Intel's Answer Express Support Suite (www.intel.com/answerexpress)—that combine backup with virus protection and technical support.

If you operate with local area networks, one person should be assigned the role of LAN administrator. One of the most important duties this person should carry out is to make periodic file backups. These backups can then be used to restore the system to a workable state following a system failure or other damaging event. The most popular (and least expensive at the time of this writing) backup device for LANs is a magnetic tape drive. Tapes can hold large volumes of information, are easy to use and store, and are generally very reliable. Most computer experts recommend that businesses keep at least three generations or more of backups, meaning that if you make a backup every week, you should have three weeks' worth of backups available. Also, it's important to note that some failures do not affect files, so plans to recover from a LAN failure must include more than file recovery. If a workstation fails in the middle of an application, there should be a procedure already mapped out as to how to recover the application and lost work.

Written along with that procedure should be an explanation of how every aspect of the LAN operates, including how to add and delete workstations and accounts. After all, your LAN administrator could become an ex-employee from one day to the next. The result could be temporary disaster for work production if written instructions aren't available.

COMPUTER CRASHES ARE INEVITABLE

DICTIONARIES OF THE FUTURE MAY DEFINE "PANIC" IN A NEW
and universal way: "experiencing computer problems while
racing to meet a deadline and discovering that telephone
technical support is practically nonexistent." Sadly, this situation goes beyond panic and into disaster for some small
businesses whose tomorrow depends upon getting the materials produced and delivered today.

Buying and maintaining the latest software is not going to
eliminate all problems. When Microsoft Windows '98 first
appeared, Microsoft helped sales by announcing that the '98
version corrected more than 5,000 bugs in Windows '95.
And that was supposed to be something to boast about?
Makes you wonder how many problems in the '98 version
the 2000 update corrects.

What to Do

During most computer crashes, the modem goes too, which
eliminates the option of seeking free help online. If not,
however, log onto the Web site of your manufacturer. Usually
you can find technical tips, updates, and answers to frequently asked questions; troubleshooting steps to try; and
downloadable solutions. Always keep the manufacturer's
Web address handy. (Find other tech support sites listed in
resources.) If the modem goes, however, then you'll need to
pick up the phone and call. This means you'll have to keep
the numbers of technical support on hand, and not stored in
your computer. Remember: When you purchase computer
equipment, you are selecting more than hardware. You also
are selecting a vendor, who should be able to help you with
problems and provide you with maintenance and support.

Windows crashes often at some small shops. To avoid
some of the more common reasons Windows will go down,
try these:

◆ Don't run too many unnecessary programs at one time.
◆ Restart your computer or workstation each day rather than
letting it run for days at a time. Of course, this will depend
on your business routines. Some businesses prefer to do
backups at night after users leave, in which case it may be

necessary for the computer to be left on. At a minimum, turn the computers off on weekends.

◆ Keep your antivirus software up to date. Look into services such as www.McAffee.com that for a monthly fee will update your software online.

◆ Check that cables and boards are connected properly.

◆ If the problem seems to be video-specific, go to your graphics board vendor's Web site for a more up-to-date driver.

◆ Visit an online fix-it location for free—but professional—advice, such as www.pcworld.com or www.microsoft.com.

CLEAN UP HARD-DRIVE SPACE

CLEANING YOUR HARD DRIVE MAY SOUND MORE LIKE A GOOD idea than a necessity, but consider how frustrating it is to discover that you're out of space just when you're working on a tight deadline.

What to Do

Start your cleaning efforts now by

◆ deleting old temporary files and archiving, compressing, or deleting old document files; and

◆ defragmenting your disk on a regular basis.

RECOVERING FROM ACCIDENTAL DELETIONS

BEING ABLE TO TYPE QUICKLY CAN ALSO MEAN THAT YOU'RE quick to find and use the delete key. Deleting a file by accident can be one of the biggest time wasters you'll ever experience because it can mean you'll have to recreate the file, if that's possible.

But it's not always human error that deletes data. According to Ontrack Data International, a Minnesota-based data recovery service, 44 percent of data is lost to mechanical failures, 14 percent to software problems, around 7 percent to viruses, and 3 percent to natural disasters, leaving only 32 percent a result of human error.

What to Do

To recover from a deletion, install Norton Utilities for Windows or Executive Software's Undelete for Windows.

Both programs work better than Windows' standard recycle bin to recover a file. If you're a start-up on a tight budget, then download Emergency Undelete at www.executive.com/undelete/eudfree/eudguest.htm. It carries fewer features than the two previous programs, but you can't beat the cost.

Another option is a highly touted data recovery product called PowerQuest's Lost & Found (www.powerquest.com). It uses a powerful search algorithm to find and restore missing data.

HOW SECURE IS YOUR COMPUTER?

SERVERS ARE GENERALLY KEPT UNDER LOCK AND KEY, BUT what about the standard desktop PC? According to Columbus, Ohio–based Safeware, the largest insurer of personal computers in the United States, an estimated 1.5 million computers were stolen, damaged, or destroyed in 1999 (the latest year for which information was available). After analyzing industrywide personal computer damage claims for a three-year period, Safeware found that 26 percent of all notebook computer losses and 25 percent of all desktop computer losses were due to theft.

Even if you find your computer still sitting on your desk after a break-in, that doesn't mean that all is necessarily safe. You may be left with little more than a shell. Let's face it, if you can easily remove and replace a hard disk drive, then other people can do it, too. Drives can be removed, copied and replaced, or worse, replaced with a different hard drive. Cyberfiends can even install software on your hard drive that records passwords, e-mail messages, and other vital information. For all these reasons, many companies use "diskless" computers, also known as dummy stations. A diskless workstation configured with a LAN does not have any local disk drives. Instead, it has its operating system boot logic in a read-only memory (ROM) chip. Although a diskless computer is fully dependent on the server for all of its software and cannot function without the network, it does offer the advantage of lower cost, better security, and tighter control for the business owner.

What to Do

Establish a policy whereby employees are required to place diskettes and tapes in locked drawers and cabinets at the end of the day. Advise them to use the keyboard lock to disable their keyboards. You could also, if feasible, require employees to use password protection for Windows and passwords for screen savers, but remind them not to leave the password within view.

The obvious and easiest line of defense is to put a lock on the door to your offices, but you may also want to install more protection. Office supply companies are now offering high-security computer cases for sale. These cases are equipped with switches that will let you know if the computer has been tampered with since you last used it. Other options include tie-down kits, complete with lock-down plates, strong adhesives, cable traps, and alarms. Most of these kits are available through your local office supply store or online suppliers.

And finally, marking your equipment may not prevent it from being stolen, but it certainly will help police distinguish it from others they retrieve each year. Mark your equipment with an ultraviolet pen; thieves won't try to remove the marking because they won't see that it is there. Also, you can get identification tags with serial numbers that permanently go on computers. Start your search for them at your local office supply or computer hardware store.

WITH E-MAIL YOU BECOME VULNERABLE

THE MOMENT YOU MAKE E-MAIL AVAILABLE TO YOUR EMPLOYees, you not only make the communication aspects of their jobs easier, you also may jeopardize the security or integrity of your company. For example, an employee could

◆ forward a message that contains a racist or sexist comment,

◆ send information to a competitor that contains confidential information,

◆ write a hasty message in anger blasting your vendors or suppliers for shoddy service, or

♦ post negative information about your company in an Internet chat room.

The courts have already said that it is legal to subpoena electronic documents to use as evidence in court, so what your employees write and send can be used against you. Also, consider the lengthy route that data follows and the many "hands" it passes through as it whirs across the Internet. This should convince you to establish a tighter policy regarding company vital information.

What to Do

Of course, you can't always prevent these situations from happening, because you can't completely control employees, but there are three things you can do to protect your company from liability in a lawsuit:

1 **Increase your liability coverage.** Make sure your liability insurance includes coverage for electronic messages. If not, increase your coverage or change policies so that you are covered. Learn more about insurance needs for the small business in Chapter 6.

2 **Establish policies.** Write down your in-house policy regarding what is and is not appropriate regarding e-mail. Explain that messages that are not clear can be misinterpreted. Require employees to refrain from writing jokes, sarcasm, offhand comments, and anything that could be interpreted as harassment, discrimination, and illegal practice. Also spell out how you want them to maintain the confidentiality of the company. End your policy statement with the advice that if they're ever in doubt, they should ask for clarification. Make sure all employees receive a copy of your policies, read them, and sign off as having read them.

3 **If you're still concerned, find out what your legal rights are in your state.** You may be able to monitor what your employees do on e-mail, so that you can periodically "watch" the activities of your employees. To learn more, contact your attorney, the state SBA office, or the National Federation of Independent Business (www.nfib.com). The laws are generally in your favor. Then, begin to check e-mail messages and watch e-mail activity from time to time.

INTERNET ACCESS BRINGS PLEASURE *AND* PAIN

IF THAT ACCESS TO E-MAIL DESCRIBED ABOVE GIVES EMPLOY-ees access to the Internet too, then your list of potential problems grows even more. In theory, if you have a Web site, then you're technically considered a publisher and are, therefore, liable for the same situations as a large publisher, including being sued for copyright infringement and plagiarism. If an employee downloads information for company use, you might be held liable.

A Web browser can be a conduit through which racist, pornographic, or hate-related information enters a company, leading to litigation. For example, employees at CitiGroup and Morgan Stanley sued their employers for the distress caused by racist jokes received over company e-mail.

Employees also can cost you countless hours of nonproductive work time as they surf the Net, shop at online stores, peruse auctions at eBay, research personal vacation options, or manage their stock portfolios. The Toledo, Ohio–based research firm NRO found that almost 50 percent of employees frequently surf the Web for personal reasons while at work.

Your biggest threat, however, may be from disgruntled employees. The name Timothy Lloyd is well known throughout the IT world. In 1996, Lloyd caused an estimated $12 million in damages to his then employer, Omega Engineering. Why? Lloyd had learned that he was about to be fired, so he planted a logic bomb that systematically erased all of Omega's contracts and the proprietary software used by the company, and tainted its Web presence. Other Timothy Lloyds exist in smaller organizations, too: As this book was being written, several watchdog Web sites were reporting about a hospital employee who, based on a mere rumor of being fired, arranged a comfortable severance package for herself by encrypting a critical patient database and added graffiti to the hospital's Web home page. In exchange for the decryption key, the hospital agreed to a significant termination bonus and not to press charges.

Of course, employees aren't a company's only concern when it comes to the Internet. There is the all-too-familiar situation in which a company finds itself the victim of lies posted on the Internet. This situation can affect not only the targeted company's profits, stock prices, sales, and reputation, but if the person who posted the false information uses an account while at work, the *employer of the perpetrator* can be in trouble, too.

Some well-known Internet attacks include the following:

◆ Fashion design Tommy Hilfiger was accused of making racist remarks on *Oprah*. It didn't matter that Hilfiger had never appeared on the show nor that he markets extensively to minorities; the information still took flight throughout the Web.

◆ Microsoft's home page was accused of being infected with a virus. Of course it wasn't.

◆ Database Lexis-Nexis was accused of selling the Social Security numbers of private citizens at a profit. It wasn't, but its reputation was tarnished anyway.

◆ McDonald's comes under attack quite often regarding additives to their meat.

◆ Mrs. Field's Cookies was accused by anti-domestic-violence activists for shipping free products to an acquittal party for O. J. Simpson. Of course the shipments never occurred.

Here, as shared by Dan Janal, president of Janal Communications (www.janal.com), and originally published at www.scambusters.org is the story of a company engaged in a long, difficult strike with its union and how it fought back against false information on the Web:

"One day, the PR manager searched for new information about the strike on a search engine. He found a site that contained several lies and pieces of misinformation, including a purported TV interview with the local anchorman and the president of the union. The transcript was totally fabricated. The interview never took place. The transcript contained misleading and false statements. However, anyone who read the page would have thought the information was true. How would they know differently? Clearly, the page had to come down.

"The PR manager called the company lawyer and began to plan a strategy. They looked at the page but couldn't find any contact information. But they looked at the source code for the page [which you can do by using the browser toolbar to "view page source" in Netscape or "view document source" in Explorer]. They didn't find a name or phone number of the person who posted the page, but they did find an e-mail address.

"They went to Dejanews, a search engine for newsgroup messages. They typed in the e-mail address and found many messages posted by that user. She was an avid poster in the cancer survivors group, the blues music group, and the weddings group. And while she hadn't put her name on the offending union Web page, she did tell everyone her name and phone number in her newsgroup messages!

"The lawyer and PR person noticed one more thing: the Web page was not posted on a union site, but on a real estate agency's site. They did a little research offline and found out that the person who posted the page worked in real estate for the company whose Web site hosted the offending pages.

"Armed with this knowledge, the lawyer called the woman. The conversation went something like this: 'Hello. We know you had breast cancer. Your favorite blues artist is B. B. King, and your daughter is getting married in July. We also know you posted a Web page filled with inaccuracies about the union. If you don't take the page down within one hour, we will call your boss, who probably will not be too happy to know you have put her license in jeopardy by posting libelous information on her Web site. We will call the state realty board and tell them you are spreading libelous information, which is probably a violation of your license. And we will call the anchorman and show him the interview you created. By the way, we copied the pages, so if we need to go to court or to the state realty board, we can.'

Within five minutes, she had taken down the page."

What to Do

The first step in protecting yourself against accusations of posting damaging material is to establish a policy that clearly states how employees can and can't use the Internet.

Be aware, however, that it's counterproductive to treat

employees as potential threats, because it hurts morale. One of the best solutions to avoiding computer tampering by employees is to take extra steps to ensure you wouldn't hire someone who would do this in the first place. Beef up recruitment practices and conduct more extensive background checks during the hiring process so that you can eliminate potential offenders. Make it known from day one that you monitor computer activity closely, and have employees read and sign a security policy. Then, if possible, share computer access codes, passwords, and vital information with two employees instead of one—that is, two employees who do not necessarily socialize outside the office. This way, you build in a simplified system of checks and balances in which one employee is regularly checking on another's work.

And finally, take cybersabotage seriously. Let employees know that you will not tolerate it and that you are on the lookout for it as closely as you are physical theft of property. (See also Chapter 2, which discusses steps for reducing crime.) The 2000 Information Security Industry Survey (as reported in *Information Security* magazine) quoted throughout this book found that the number of organizations in which employees intentionally disclosed or destroyed proprietary corporate information increased by 41 percent from 1998 to 1999. Even though this survey reflects a strong emphasis on big business, small-business specialists believe that the results reflect small business as well since most small organizations do not have multilayered security infrastructures that make it harder to adulterate critical information. For example, according to Computer Security Institute (CSI), an insider attack cost the target enterprise about $2.7 million on average, but an outsider attack cost only about $57,000 on average.

As for material being posted *against* your company, you will have to accept that this can happen and that there is rarely anything you can do to prevent it. The Internet has given a means to cyberfinks to voice their gripes, people who would otherwise stay quiet. Unfortunately, these people can use fake names and addresses to conceal their identity, often making it impossible for companies to do anything about the information. Equally discouraging is the fact that information on the Web is often considered reliable because it looks reliable. Web sites and stories give the appearance of journalism but without the sweat, tedious fact checking, reliable sources, and weighing of objective opinions that ethical journalism offers. An attacker can say what he pleases without being held accountable because there is no journalistic imperative for him to check facts, nor is there an editorial staff demanding it, as there is for other media.

Janal outlines these seven steps for protecting your company:

1 **Assign someone to monitor newsgroups and search engines at least once a week.** Check for company names and product names. If your company is very visible, check the names of the CEO or president as well.

2 **If you find postings in newsgroups, read all the messages about the subject and determine whether you need to respond.** In some cases, the issue dies. Or smarter posters call the source to verify his information.

3 **If you think you need to respond to set the record straight, do so.** Newsgroup netiquette forbids advertising in newsgroups, but not the honest exchange of information. In fact, if you don't state your side of the story, people might assume that silence is assent.

4 **Contact the source directly and see if you can work out the problem.** Maybe there was some miscommunication that went haywire. Most people can be reasonable. In fact, some of the biggest patrons for companies are people who once had customer service problems that were set straight. Before you call or write, see if the person posted other messages in other newsgroups. Dejanews provides links to all messages the person posted. If you read the messages, you might begin to see how you can develop rapport with that person.

5 **If you find a rogue Web site, see if you can talk to the site owner and find out what the problem is.** If the owner received bad customer service or bought a faulty product, take note: this person might speak for many people who have had

similar problems with your company. In this case, your problem is really an internal problem. If you straighten out the problem, the rogue site will probably die out. If you don't, the page will live forever, like U.S. Worst, an attack page for U.S. West, the telecommunications giant. People can post their own horror stories on the site; for a while, visitors could even find out the home phone number of the chairman of the company so they could complain directly to him.

6 **It is hard to challenge rogue Web site owners because they are protected by the First Amendment, which guarantees freedom of speech.** However, they are subject to the same laws of libel as in the real world. So if they are spreading false information and they know it is false, then you could bring suit to shut them down.

7 **Be sure to copy the pages onto your computer and print them out on paper.** This is your evidence. If you don't and the posters remove the offending material, you won't have any proof of the libel. Programs like WebWhacker and WebBuddy can copy entire sites, including the text, pictures, and HTML.

BE ON THE LOOKOUT FOR SCAMS

WE'VE ALL HEARD THE EXPRESSION "DON'T BELIEVE EVERYthing you read." Nowhere is this more true than when it comes to material on the Web. On the other hand, the Web offers many fortuitous deals and opportunities that you won't find elsewhere. How can you trust that what you read is true?

What to Do

Follow your instinct. If a deal seems too good to be true, then it probably is. However, to be sure, visit these sites for the latest scam alerts:

◆ About.com—specifically its Urban Legends and Folklore feature—(www.about.com)

◆ Better Business Bureau Online (www.bbb.org)

◆ Coalition Against Unsolicited Commercial E-mail (www.cauce.org)

◆ Federal Trade Commission's Consumer Protection Unit

(www.ftc.gov/ftc/consumer.htm)
- ◆ Fight Spam on the Internet (spam.abuse.net)
- ◆ Internet Scambusters (www.scambusters.com)
- ◆ National Consumers League
  (www.natlconsumersleague.org)
- ◆ National Fraud Information Center (www.fraud.org)
- ◆ SpamCop (spamcop.net)

YOU DON'T HAVE A WEB PRESENCE

IT'S HARD TO IMAGINE ANY BUSINESS NOT HAVING A
presence on the Web, but I still meet business owners from
time to time who are convinced that they don't need a Web
site. Their clientele, they argue, is made up of local residents;
they offer a service or product that the consumer can only
get by visiting their store or shop—for example, a customer
having his tires rotated, his car detailed, or his hair cut. However, I would argue that there are several auto service centers
and stylists' shops in most small towns. The day will come
(quickly) when consumers will comparison shop on the Web
rather than by calling around town to get prices. After all,
this is the standard way of living that teenagers—your future
customers—are learning right now. Without a Web presence, a small business won't even be in the running.

As for retail establishments that don't have a Web site, I
find their thinking shortsighted and not in line with forward-
thinking management. In almost every area the Web has
touched (and what hasn't it touched?), consumers have been
able to benefit from lower prices. Anyone who is not convinced that a Web presence is necessary will soon learn that
customers' loyalty will falter in direct proportion to the savings they can realize by shopping on the Web.

The lower overhead of pared-down Internet retail businesses allows them to pass the savings on to the buyer. This
means that the only selling edges traditional stores have are
lack of shipping expenses and one-on-one customer service.
If you're still not convinced how vital a Web site will be to
your future, then consider this: consumer purchases over
the Web will rise from $4.5 billion in 1998 to $35.3 billion
by 2002, according to eMarketer, a New York City company

that tracks Internet marketing trends and statistics online.

Knowing where technology is headed could have positive influences on the way you develop your business. As I write this book, airlines are offering customers the opportunity to surf the Web from their seats, and GM is planning to equip vehicles with a satellite service that will act as a mobile Internet service provider. In short, the Internet is omnipresent and should be a reality you factor into your business if you want to remain competitive.

What to Do

Find out what your competitors are doing on the Web. Then broaden the search and find out what other businesses in other parts of the country are doing. Contact them. Ask them what's working and what's not. When you get an idea of what works for them, establish your own unique Web presence. Then, include your Web URL on all written materials.

PROTECT YOUR WEB PRESENCE

ACCORDING TO *WORKING WOMAN* MAGAZINE (MAY 2000, page 46), the Bush campaign registered fifty-four domain names when George W. Bush was running for president in 2000. And no wonder: they had discovered a parody site that was set up under www.gwbush.com that not only looked official but sold buttons featuring Bush with a silver spoon up his nose and text that read: "It's the hypocrisy, stupid." Meanwhile, the Gore campaign discovered that www.allgore.com featured a fictional candidate named All Gore who wanted to eliminate automobiles in cities with over 50,000 total population and help communities outlaw chewing gum. This hacking and defacing continued through election-day morning, when visitors to the Republican National Committee's Web site were surprised to find a 1,000-word pro-Gore plea, complete with a link to Gore's Web site.

Countless companies, too, have been the target of parody or insult sites. For example, visit www.Untied.com and you'll find a site dedicated to blasting United Airlines. Companies are learning that they need to register more than just their own Web site if they want to protect their name from poachers, disgruntled customers, and competitors.

What to Do

Protect your company name:

◆ Register the plural and singular versions.
◆ Register it with the word "the" in front of the name.
◆ Register hyphenated versions if it's a compound name.
◆ Register misspellings (such "Untied" for United, as mentioned above)
◆ Register all three extensions: .com, .net, and .org.
◆ Link all these registrations to the home page on your "real" URL.

I can speak from personal experience on this lesson. When my partner and I founded our Internet writing institute, www.WriteDirections.com, years ago, we only registered one name (do you remember those days of Internet naivete?). After it was too late, we discovered that a freelance writer had the name www.WriteDirection.com, and to add insult to injury, her first name is Debra. I often wonder how many clients we send her way and how many give up when they discover the site is not what they thought they would get.

YOUR WEB SITE HOSTING COMPANY CRASHES

IMAGINE SENDING A CATALOG IN THE MAIL TO MORE THAN 60 million people offering them free shipping for a specified time if they order from your Web site. Now imagine that when they try to take advantage of the offer within that designated time, the site is inaccessible. If your tarnished image wouldn't send your heart racing, then the cost of the catalogs and mailing probably would. This situation happened to Toys "R" Us in late 1999. And similar problems have happened to countless other Web-based companies—for example, eBay, with its more than 3 million customers, has had to shut down several times, once for more than twenty hours. Even Amazon.com has been inaccessible at times. Sites crash and fail for several reasons: server failure, programming errors, software prob-

lems, human error, and more. Small businesses are especially vulnerable to crashes because they generally are
involved with a Web hosting company that offers a shared-
server environment.

(€ What to Do

While it's impossible to be 100 percent safe, it is possible to
find hosting companies that are more reliable than others. If
you can afford dedicated hosting, which means that the host
company dedicates a server to your company alone, then do
it. Many small businesses can't do this, however, because
fees start at $1,500 per month. Therefore, one option is to go
shopping at the Web Host Guild, www.whg.org, which states
as its mission "to protect consumers from unscrupulous
hosts, and to help identify the honest, legitimate host companies that exist." To be a member, host companies must earn
certification.

When you talk with a host company, ask a lot of questions.
Don't assume that they all work the same. Ask if your Web
site will be protected by two servers so that if one crashes, all
your traffic will be routed to the other one. Ask if your Web
site will be monitored every day, and how. Ask for a description of a backup plan in case there is a problem.

YOUR WEB SITE DURING A CRISIS: PEOPLE *WILL* COME

IF YOU WISH THAT MORE PEOPLE WOULD VISIT YOUR WEB
site, then be careful what you wish for. One way to ensure
they'll come is to experience a crisis. When your company
is in trouble or rumors are spreading about you, people
will want to "check you out," perhaps for the first time.
This means that you had better be able to handle the extra
attention.

(€ What to Do

If visitors can send messages, ask questions, and make
requests, then you will need more people to handle responses. Put one person in charge of all responses, and have that
person police the site. He or she can hand out messages for

other people to answer. Just be sure the answers are consistent and get your message out.

If something on the site is part of the problem, then you will need to be able to remove it quickly. If it takes you a long time to get something new posted on the site, making changes will not go much faster during a crisis situation. Find out what your options are. This advice also applies to marketing material on the site about a service or product that experiences a crisis. You certainly don't want to keep advertising the safety of a particular baby stroller if you have just found yourself in legal trouble because three children have been severely injured from their runaway strollers. The best action to take in this instance is to remove the information about the defective product and replace it with a news release describing your reaction to the crisis and what you plan to do.

And finally, no doubt you adhered to good Web writing techniques when preparing the site, by adding language that spoke to visitors one-on-one; so keep the same language when presenting messages of a negative nature, too. Let your human touch show through. Your "crisis" material will be a jarring contrast to the "friendly" news at the site if it's filled with corporate lingo.

YOUR WEB SITE DURING A CRISIS: PEOPLE *WON'T* COME

A DIFFERENT KIND OF CRISIS OCCURS WHEN A HOAX HAS BEEN passed around warning people away from your site. This happened to Blue Mountain Arts, a small family-owned publishing house of greeting cards, poetry books, and electronic cards, in early 1999 when the following message was passed around the Internet:

"Subject: Fwd: Blue Mountain Cards Virus
"ALERT!!!
"Date: Sat, 27 Feb 1999
"Just received a call from family. A friend of theirs opened a card from Blue Mountain cards and system crashed. Do not open Blue Mountain cards until further notice."

As virus warnings do, this one took on a life of its own as, internationally, people forwarded it to everyone they knew, posted it to newsgroups and list servers, and talked about it over the watercooler. In retrospect, computer experts say it was foolish for anyone to think that Blue Mountain's cards could have carried a virus, since they are nothing more than graphics and text and carry no attachments. Sadly, for Blue Mountain, this was a case of perception not matching reality, and the perception dictated the flow of the negative message.

What to Do

Respond! Quickly! Blue Mountain founder Stephen Schutz posted a statement on the site that the rumor was a hoax and that the site was completely safe. Simultaneously, son Jared began talking to the news media.

Of course, it will help if you can find out what started the rumor; then you will have more meaty material to present to the news media. In the Blue Mountain incident, son Jared had to assume the negative message started as a result of sabotage. At the time, he was quoted at www.About.com saying, "To grow the speed it has grown, I strongly suspect that a person or persons are actively spamming this warning around .... We are at wits' end about how to fight this unseen enemy."

What also might have helped the Schutzes would have been posting their own messages with newsgroups and list servers and collecting instances of other Web hoaxes so that the news media could build an even stronger story. With more examples, the Schutzes' request for coverage to squelch the rumor wouldn't have seemed as self-serving.

HACKERS CAN SEVERELY CRIPPLE A BUSINESS

IF THE COMPUTER SYSTEMS AT THE PENTAGON, THE REPUBLI-can National Committee, and the *New York Times* can be the victims of break-ins by computer hackers, what makes you think it couldn't happen to you? Hackers can be frightening people for your business, because they're not necessarily anonymous individuals who want to break in and steal credit card information; instead they're often a business's own employees, consultants, contractors, or disgruntled contacts who have an axe to grind. In one case affecting the *New York*

Times, the hackers wanted a forum in which to complain that a fellow hacker had been jailed and treated unfairly by a *Times* reporter.

Fortunately for the *Times,* the hacking job was obvious, so it was quickly found and corrected. But it may not be obvious to you if you are the victim; a hacker could change just a few vital numbers at your site, or forward a plagiarized or damaging e-mail from your account, or steal information to pass on—or sell—to a competitor. Other highly damaging hacking tricks include sabotaging files, inserting viruses, and erasing files.

What to Do

There are several steps you can take to cut down on the likelihood of damage from a hacker.

◆ Don't leave your computers connected to the Internet needlessly. If you must, then chances are you will not be able to monitor your computer yourself, so hire a company to do it for you. A managed security service will monitor your computer twenty-four hours a day, seven days a week, for fees at or below $50 per year. Just do a Web search—there are thousands of companies available. But note: get names of their customers and call to verify that the company does what it says it will.

◆ Install fire wall security (a mix of software and hardware designed to keep out unauthorized Internet users). While you're at it, make sure the ISP hosting your Web site has a fire wall. Hackers can gain access through holes in your Web server. A fire wall will monitor the flow of information between your Web server and the Internet, then block any unwanted communication. Microsoft offers a security site that is filled with tips regarding security. Find it at www. microsoft.com/security and others in the resources at the end of this book.

◆ Watch your employees closely. That 1998 survey reported earlier from PricewaterhouseCoopers and *Information Week* found that of the companies they surveyed that had experienced a security breach within that year, 58 percent of the break-ins were by employees.

◆ Make good backups of all data so that if something does get hacked, you have a quick way to restore service.

◆ Keep credit information encrypted and stored elsewhere.

◆ Report the theft so that employees and other observers see that you take action rather than just chalk it up to a lesson learned for next time. This may indeed prevent it from happening again. To report a theft, start with your local police. They may refer you to higher authorities, depending upon the damage amount, the type of crime, and the nature of information stolen or tainted.

SOFTWARE LICENSES: PIRATING IS ILLEGAL

OTHER THAN HOW TO USE IT, ONE OF THE MOST IMPORTANT things you should know about your software is its licensing agreement. It's illegal to pirate software and share it among users in an office. Several companies and a major state university have been found guilty of illegally copying software and have been heavily fined.

Although there are no standards when it comes to license agreements (which just compounds the problem), there generally is one universal rule you have to follow: you do not get ownership of the software you purchase; you are simply given the right to use it. This means that you must adhere to the rights of use as spelled out in the agreement. When you purchase software, it's generally encased in an envelope. On that envelope is printed a notice alerting you to the fact that if you open the envelope, then you agree to the stipulations of the license.

What to Do

Become familiar with the terms of your licensing agreements. You receive them with every purchase of software because they establish the terms of ownership and use. Failure to comply with the terms sets a poor example for your employees. It's hard to expect honesty and integrity from your workers if you don't practice it yourself.

Also, any employee found using pirated software—whether or not you provided it—subjects your company to a potential lawsuit. Make sure your employees know of your strong stance on this issue. This means that unless you purchase the options for multiple users, then software is for a single user or single workstation, not multiples. Also be forewarned that the install process often counts and reports the number of installations. If you want vendor support, you need to respect your license agreements.

ERGONOMICS CAN TAKE YOU ALL THE WAY TO COURT

ALSO KNOWN AS HUMAN ENGINEERING, ERGONOMICS IS THE process of designing equipment to maximize worker production and to relieve discomfort while using the equipment. Physical problems such as headaches, neck and eye strain, radiation side effects, and muscle and tendon problems have all been associated with working with certain computers and monitors, especially VDTs (video display terminals).

 What to Do

As a business owner, you may not be to blame for any negative repercussions arising from using the equipment in your offices, but you could be held responsible in court. Make sure your office offers the best in ergonomic conditions for your employees: adequate lighting, proper support when sitting, appropriately adjusted monitors, detachable keyboards that can be moved for comfort when working, etc. Periodically do a walk-around to inspect user work areas. Talk to employees and have them voice their satisfaction with their equipment and environment in front of others.

Also, follow legislation regarding ergonomics to make sure you always comply with the law. As I write this, OSHA is busy formalizing an ergonomics policy for home-based work. A recent OSHA news release announced that home offices will not be inspected for violations of federal safety and health rules. However, the agency will, when asked, follow up on complaints involving potentially hazardous factory work being performed in the home. Examples include assembling electronics, using unguarded crimping machines, or handling potentially hazardous materials without adequate protection.

CREDIT CARD FRAUD

CREDIT CARD FRAUD IS RIFE IN E-COMMERCE AND IS PRO-
jected to get worse as Internet use expands rapidly in the
future. The fear for entrepreneurs is that, as merchants, they
are responsible for every credit card transaction they accept.
Eventually, if they accept enough phony transactions, they
can reach what is considered a high incidence of fraud. Web
merchants who have reached as little as 1 percent charge-
back rates have been barred by card issuing companies from
accepting credit cards at all. If you lose your privileges to
accept cards, you could find yourself out of business.

"Repeated charge-backs to card companies suggest that
your business isn't viable or legitimate," says Audri G. Lanford, an Internet scams expert and coeditor of the newsletter
Internet ScamBusters (www.scambusters.org). "Your business will be perceived with skepticism and negativity if you
demonstrate many repeat problems."

Reducing credit card fraud can save you time, reputation,
and revenue. According to Lanford, "There has been a
tremendous increase in the number of merchants who have
been scammed by crooks who place fraudulent orders using
stolen credit card information." Lanford explains that
because merchants are not provided the same protection as
consumers when it comes to credit card fraud, it behooves
them to take the eight steps below. These steps can also be
found at Lanford's site (www.scambusters.org/creditcard-
fraud.html):

1 Take extra steps to validate each order. Don't accept orders
unless complete information is provided, including full
address and phone number.

2 Be wary of orders with different "bill to" and "ship to"
addresses. Require anyone who uses a different "ship to"
address to send a fax with their signature and credit card
number authorizing the transaction.

3 Be especially cautious of orders that come from free
e-mail services—there is a much higher incidence of fraud
from these services because it's easy for a scamster to open a
free, anonymous e-mail account in another person's name
and then send the merchant an order using the fake e-mail

account and a fraudulent credit card number. Many businesses won't even accept orders that come through these free e-mail accounts anymore; you may be wise to follow suit.

What precautions should you take with orders from free e-mail accounts? Send an e-mail requesting additional information before you process the order. More specifically, ask for a non-free e-mail address, the name and phone number of the bank that issued the credit card, the exact name on the credit card, and the exact billing address. Often, you won't get a reply, according to Lanford. If you do, you can easily verify the information (which you should take the time to do).

4 Be wary of orders that are larger than your typical order amount, and orders with next-day delivery. Crooks don't care what it costs, since they aren't planning on paying for it anyway.

5 Pay extra attention to international orders. Do everything you can to validate the order before you ship your product to a different country.

6 If you're suspicious, pick up the phone and call the customer to confirm the order using the phone number that's listed with the billing address of the cardholder.

7 Consider using software or services to fight credit card fraud online, such as Cybersource and Clear Commerce Corp.

8 If you as a merchant have the misfortune of being scammed by a credit card thief, contact your merchant processor immediately. You should also contact your bank and the police. The police will probably take a report but may not do much else depending on the dollar amount of the fraud.

Take a Deep Breath

SURE, WHEN IT COMES TO YOUR COMPUTER NETWORK, SEVeral truths prevail: computer equipment and links to the outside world are necessary, the security risk is great, something will inevitably malfunction, small businesses have the hardest time getting help, and the difficulties will only intensify in the future. There's no denying it: the growth of computer technology has created an entire new industry of crime. However, as this chapter points out, a little preventive medicine can go a long way toward

Secure Your Vital Records

YOUR COMPANY MAINTAINS a lot of paperwork and records necessary for the continuation and recovery of your business following a crisis. Make sure that you have copied, backed up, or in some way secured these important records:

◆ deeds/leases
◆ permits
◆ copyrights
◆ vendor and client contracts
◆ tax records
◆ personnel files
◆ engineering drawings
◆ material safety data sheets
◆ compliance documentation for government regulatory agencies
◆ any document that legally needs to be saved for a certain period of time
◆ work in progress that is not backed up because it is not yet finished
◆ claims files, litigation files
◆ financial information, stock and shareholder information
◆ corporate policy manual
◆ company charter
◆ employee handbook
◆ up-to-date copy of phone numbers, computer and Internet logon codes and passwords, employee phone numbers, and company credit card numbers
◆ your computer's basic operating system, boot files, and critical software
◆ invoices, shipping lists, and other documentation of your computer system configuration

173

helping you rest a little easier at night.

Now, catch your breath; we're going to move on to Chapter 6, where you'll learn how to add the right layer of insurance to your security efforts.

Insure for the Worst with the Best Coverage Available

ET'S ADMIT IT: SHOPPING FOR BUSINESS insurance is about as appealing as shopping for a box of tarantulas. Perhaps you're thinking of flipping past the next several pages and skipping this chapter altogether.

But don't. With this chapter, my intent is to remove the glaze from your eyes that, if you're like other small-business owners, always seems to set in the moment the word *insurance* is uttered.

I know firsthand that most small-business owners don't like researching, reviewing, and buying insurance. To them, it's like a tax—a necessary but burdensome expense that should be kept to a minimum. That's how I viewed it, too, until I collected experience in my work as a crisis management consultant and saw how insurance coverage could benefit an organization beyond the obvious advantage of providing money for restoration following a peril.

Besides reducing the uncertainties under which you do business—which in itself generally provides a better night's sleep—insurance can reduce employee turnover, make you more attractive to potential investors, enhance your credit rating at the bank, and convince wary customers that you're worth doing business with. So if you can begin to look at insurance as an investment in your business and its future, then the task of identifying and shopping for insurance becomes a little less burdensome and annoying.

Become a Risk Manager

THROUGHOUT THIS BOOK, YOU'VE HAD TO WEAR MANY hats: owner, manager, director of human resources, IT specialist, and outside observer, to name a few. Now you have to assume the role of risk manager.

Large companies generally employ risk managers to analyze possible exposures to loss or liability. It's their job to safeguard the company against accidental and preventable loss and to minimize the financial consequences of unavoidable losses. To do this, risk managers have to choose the best way to deal with potential losses. Since you own a small business, you probably can't afford to hire a risk manager, so you'll have to do it yourself.

In Chapter 1, I said that one way to handle the risks that you face is to transfer them. As a risk manager, you can do that by buying insurance, which transfers some or all of the risk to the insurance company. You pay a premium rather than taking the risk of not protecting yourself against the possibility of a much larger financial loss. Sounds great; but then there are those business owners who buy too much insurance and end up cash poor from paying high premiums for what often turns out to be the wrong type of insurance anyway. "It can get confusing if you don't take the time to do a little research in advance," says Don Urbanciz, CEO of www.insurancenoodle.com. "It's been our experience that small businesses are overinsured as often as they are underinsured, especially when it comes to property insurance."

But is all this advance work worth the time? You bet it is, according to Urbanciz: "Insurable losses emanating from small businesses in the commercial property and casualty spectrum average about $25 to $35 billion per year," he says. Besides serving as an online insurance broker catering to small commercial businesses, www.insurancenoodle.com keeps abreast of trends and research in the insurance industry. The site offers a glossary of insurance terms, so you may want to start your education there.

Do Some Research

IN BUSINESS INSURANCE AS IN PERSONAL INSURANCE, YOU alone decide which risks you must insure against, although some coverage is required by law, such as workers' compensation. As an employer, you must provide state-mandated coverage for injuries and illnesses that are job related through workers' compensation insurance.

Groups pertinent to your business may mandate that still other risks be covered; for example, if you have a loan on property, the lender generally requires you to be insured. If you cancel that insurance, the lender may have the right to foreclose on the property or purchase insurance itself and charge you a higher price for it. Overall, however, insurance is generally "good to have" rather than "required to have." This knowledge tends to make the shopping a little less intimidating and overwhelming. Now, having said that, let me add my own opinion and caution: insurance is a "must have." Thanks to the litigious society we live in, your business should be insured at all times for property, equipment, and inventory, as well as against your potential liabilities.

You will read a review of the most common types of insurance in a moment, but first let me address insurance carriers: Many small business owners set themselves up to experience stress when it comes to purchasing insurance because they let the same person who sells insurance also be the person who *educates* them about what insurance they need. The drawbacks in this situation are obvious. Even a search on the Web will result in hundreds of thousands of sites that provide primers on insurance, but a closer look will reveal that many of these sites are affiliated with one insurance carrier and, therefore, may not be able to give you options.

Urbanciz, whose company is typical of what you should look for since it aligns itself with at least a half dozen carriers, advises that small-business owners make sure that potential agents understand their business. "That may seem obvious, but too often buyers—and the agents themselves—assume that the agents understand the business. Every business has different exposures. If you run a florist shop, you will have different risks than someone down the street who operates a card shop. A florist is going to be concerned about what happens if they lose refrigeration. A card shop owner certainly won't care about that."

Let's Get Started

FIRST YOU'LL WANT TO DETERMINE HOW TO TRANSFER YOUR
risks, how much to transfer, and how much you're willing
to pay to do so, so that you are armed with information
when you approach a potential insurer. To arm yourself,
you'll need some understanding of the basic types of insurance, which I'll share in a moment, and an idea of how to
keep your costs down. Let's look at the latter idea first.
When you begin strategizing your insurance purchases,
keep the following in mind:

◆ Look at the lists you created in Chapter 1 and decide how
much loss you might suffer from each risk. Prioritize them
and decide which risks you want to insure against.

◆ Cover your largest risk exposure first, then move on to secondary risks. Don't try to save money by ignoring the latter,
however. If you think that a risk has a low probability of
occurring, then it will probably carry a low premium, too.

◆ Avoid duplication of insurance to keep your costs low.

◆ Shop first for an insurance agent/carrier through any of the
professional organizations you belong to. Since each industry has its own unique ways of doing business, it only makes
sense that it will have its own unique perils, too. Professional
associations may have discounted insurance packages tailored to your industry.

◆ Buy in as large a unit as possible. Many package policies are
suitable to particular types of businesses, and if yours is one
of those businesses, then it might be your best option. Often,
these packages are the only way a small business can get adequate protection.

◆ Select one agent/carrier to handle your insurance. Having
more than one may weaken responsibility when it comes
time to tap into that insurance. Besides, even if you have several policies on your property, for example, you can still collect only the amount of your actual loss.

◆ Don't withhold important information from your insurance
carrier about your business and its risks. Your agent/carrier
should be your professional and confidential helper.

◆ Tell your agent/carrier of the steps you are taking to prevent loss. Explain all preventive steps you've adopted from this book. Describe your ignition cutoff systems, alarms, security and fire-protection systems, even your emergency response plans; for example, some insurance carriers offer a discount on business interruption insurance if your company has a place where it can operate in the event of a fire or other crisis.

◆ Seek out as high a deductible as you can afford. Sometimes taking a higher deductible will result in a reduced premium.

Types of Insurance

IT WOULD BE IMPOSSIBLE TO OUTLINE HERE EXACTLY WHAT insurance your specific small business needs because it will vary depending on your location, type of business, and the vulnerabilities that are unique to your business. However, so that you have an overview to work from when you talk to an agent, I've included basic descriptions below. Remember that the items listed are generally covered by the type of insurance listed; always verify with your agent/carrier to be sure.

PROPERTY INSURANCE

SMALL-BUSINESS PROPERTY INSURANCE COVERS YOUR PHYSI-cal assets: buildings, equipment, inventory, furnishings, fixtures, and so on, or improvements you've made if you lease. This insurance covers a range of perils, from fire to windstorms to vandalism to some water damage.

Although most property inside insured buildings is covered, make sure any policy you're considering includes your computers and phone system. Some insurers consider these to be "special" property and require additional coverage.

When it comes to property insurance, floods are usually not covered. If you live in a flood zone, you will probably have to buy separate insurance for this risk through the National Flood Insurance Program. Be aware that the federal government requires buildings in flood zones that don't conform to floodplain building codes to be torn down if damage exceeds 50 percent of the market value, according to the Insurance Information Institute (www.iii.org). Therefore, you may want to consider purchasing ordinance or law coverage to help pay for the extra costs of tearing down the structure and rebuilding it were a flood to occur. Don't assume that just because a flood has never happened before, it never will. Flooding patterns are changed by development: water that runs off new streets and parking lots may overwhelm nearby streams and surrounding land. Landslides and sinkholes may develop because of distant earth movement, natural or man-made. The creek by your building may be a tiny, placid stream that has never flooded, but a downpour might change it into a destructive torrent that destroys your building foundation. Plan for the worst.

The Independent Insurance Agents of America offers the following checklist of property items that you can review when discussing insurance with a potential agent/carrier:

- buildings and other structures, leased or owned
- furniture, equipment, and supplies
- data processing equipment and media, including computers
- phone equipment
- inventory
- money and securities
- records of accounts receivable
- improvements you made to the premises
- machinery
- valuable papers, books, and documents
- mobile property, such as automobiles, trucks, and construction equipment
- satellite dishes
- boilers
- signs, fences, and other outdoor property not attached to a building

According to Urbanciz, when it comes to shopping for property insurance, "Be sure you're working with a current appraisal, and look at replacement cost, not market value." He also says that if you're a wholesaler, retailer, or seasonal business, then you should remember that your inventory will fluctuate. His advice: "Think of your value of inventory at the highest time of the year and work with that."

LIABILITY

THIS INSURANCE WILL PROTECT YOUR COMPANY IF IT IS SUED, including lawsuits from accidents that cause bodily injury (a customer slips on your icy steps), accidents that cause property damage (you sell defective area rugs that "bleed" dye onto customers' hardwood floors or carpets), and a list of miscellaneous claims (like slander or false advertising). Generally, liability insurance will pay not only the cost of the damages but also the attorney fees and other costs associated with your defense in a lawsuit. However, according to the Insurance Information Institute, liability insurance will not protect you against claims due to nonperformance of a contract, wrongful termination of employees, sexual harassment, or race and gender lawsuits. (Usually, another type of insurance, sometimes known as Employment Practices Liability Insurance, can protect your business against employment-related claims, such as sexual harassment.)

Liability insurance generally can be broken down into three types:

◆ **General liability** protects you against unintentional injuries to people who visit your office.

◆ **Professional liability** pays for claims for damages resulting from the performance of your services. This insurance is for anyone who could be sued for malpractice, from hairdressers to accountants, and covers for negligence or errors and omissions that injure clients.

◆ **Product liability** pays for claims for injury or damage resulting from the use of your insured product. Any company that produces a product should have product liability insurance, but especially if that product is food, clothing, or toys.

If you're unsure how much liability insurance to buy, check for recommendations from your industry support associations.

When shopping for liability coverage, ask lots of questions. For example, under certain conditions, your business may be subject to bodily injury or property damage claims even from trespassers. And in some situations, even if a suit against you is false or fraudulent, the liability insurer pays court costs and legal fees. If you are found liable, the insurer will pay interest on judgments in addition to the liability judgments themselves.

WORKERS' COMPENSATION

DEPENDING UPON THE STATE YOU LIVE IN, WORKERS' COMP may be required if you have three or more employees. It can cover medical expenses and income replacement for employees injured on the job.

Some other types of insurance—although not absolutely essential—will greatly add to the security of your business.

BUSINESS INTERRUPTION

IF YOUR COMPANY CANNOT PROVIDE ITS PRODUCT OR SERvice, this insurance pays for the loss you incur. It does not pay for damage causing the interruption; instead, this is covered by hazard-related insurance. But it may help you meet payrolls, pay vendors, and purchase inventory until you are in full operation again. Generally, this coverage pays for the net profit (or loss) before taxes plus continuing normal operating expenses.

Business interruption insurance will replace lost income, pay ongoing expenses, and pay costs involved in getting you set up in a temporary facility so that you can continue operation. It covers the profits you would have earned, based on your financial records, had the disaster not occurred. It also covers operating expenses that continue, like electricity, even though business activities have come to a temporary halt, according to the Insurance Information Institute.

EXTRA EXPENSE

REIMBURSES YOUR COMPANY FOR A REASONABLE SUM OF money that it spends over and above normal operating expenses to avoid shutting down following a business crisis or interruption. Generally, the damage must be caused by an insured peril. Examples include rent for temporary office space and equipment, moving and hauling to that location, and some employee expenses. Usually this type of insurance will only be paid if the extra expenses help to decrease business interruption costs.

Extra expense insurance pays for temporary use of people and machinery too, all with the intent that you be able to resume operations quickly. You may want to consider extra expense insurance to pay for salaries of key employees when they become temporarily out of work due to a mishap at your company. This could prevent them from leaving you to work for competitors.

UMBRELLA

IT'S GOOD TO HAVE EXTRA LIABILITY COVERAGE WHEN THE limits on your other policies are reached. You can often purchase several hundred thousand to more than a million dollars worth of extra coverage for as little as a few hundred dollars, because the umbrella insurer is betting you'll never exceed your basic policy limits. It's for this reason, and the extra protection it provides, that Urbanciz calls umbrella coverage "sleep insurance."

COMMERCIAL AUTOMOBILE

THE VEHICLES YOU USE FOR BUSINESS PURPOSES SHOULD BE covered. Although commercial automobile insurance covers physical damage to the car, it does not cover the contents of the car; therefore, make sure your property policy covers loss outside your business.

If business use of your personal car is minimal, the necessary coverage can probably be included in your personal policy.

EMPLOYMENT PRACTICES

PROVIDE COVERAGE FOR THE POSSIBILITY OF AN EMPLOYEE suing your company for sexual harassment, wrongful termination, job discrimination, or any of the other increasingly popular claims alleging failures in your employment practices. It enables you to mount a legal defense and, if necessary, pay a settlement or damages. According to insurance carriers, this coverage did not even exist ten years ago; now it's widely available and widely needed, thanks to our litigious society.

Of course, there are many other types of insurance available, from crime insurance to glass insurance (covers all risk to plate-glass windows and showcases) to key-employee insurance. Your best bet is to review your needs with your agent/carrier to learn the options for your specific industry and company. But be sure to take along the list of risks you developed in Chapter 1; for example, unless you mention the risk of your laptop being stolen from your hotel room while traveling, you might not think to ask for separate coverage (Electronic Data Processing Insurance). Or in the midst of talking property insurance, you might forget that your biggest concern is an employee stealing from you by falsifying bookkeeping entries; in that case, you might not get around to discussing "Employee Dishonesty Coverage." Or what about "Product Liability Coverage" to protect your hair salon in case a client develops a rash after using a product you sold? Or what about "Customer Property Coverage" in case an employee steals a valuable from your client's home? The list of possible perils and their coverage goes on.

A word of caution: Business Owners Policies, known as BOPs, have been created specifically for small businesses. These are insurance policies that have bundled together property and liability coverage to allow you to obtain broad coverage with affordable premiums. However, these policies can lack flexibility when it comes to tailoring them to your business. Be forewarned that you may need to add coverage for conditions not covered by a BOP, especially when it comes to liability.

Repeating the Process

AS MUCH AS WE WOULD LIKE IT TO BE, INSURANCE IS NOT A buy-once-and-forget-about-it purchase. You need to do an annual review of your needs and your coverage, although Urbanciz says that seeking new quotes and comparison shopping for new insurance can be conducted every three to five years.

If you decide to switch companies during your annual

review, then read the new policies before making the change. Don't assume that a classification or a category in one policy carries the same meaning or intent in another policy.

Your Home-Based Business

ACCORDING TO THE INSURANCE INFORMATION INSTITUTE, the typical home owners policy provides only $2,500 coverage for business equipment. This is usually not enough to cover all the business property, let alone coverage for liability or business interruption.

In this situation, you have choices: endorsements to the home owners policy (which typically will double your standard home owners policy limits), an in-home business policy (generally provides business property coverage up to $10,000, along with liability coverage), or a business owners package policy (BOP), as described earlier.

The bottom line when it comes to insurance is to know what could happen to you, then insure for the worst and hope for the best.

When *the* Crisis Moves *from* In-House *to the* Public

SECT

ION

CHAPTER 7

Brace Yourself for Negative Publicity and Public Scrutiny

YOU KNOW YOU'RE GOING TO HAVE A BAD day when you arrive at work and a news crew is waiting in your lobby. According to small-business owners who've been there, your next thoughts run something like this: "Did someone die? Did we break a law? Violate a contract? Were we caught in a lie? Is our product defective? What did our employees do? How will I make it through this and keep my company intact? How can I find out what happened?"

Your next realization is that you are unprepared to handle the situation. In contrast, the hungry, deadline-driven reporters in your lobby are overly prepared and are already behind schedule. You break into a sweat and brace yourself for their questions, knowing that the first things said travel the farthest. With a sinking feeling, you recall a journalist once telling you, "It's our job to comfort the afflicted and afflict the comfortable." You frown as you mourn the loss of your comfort and face the affliction.

This heart-in-your-throat moment is exactly when you will wish you had prepared in advance to deal with unexpected situations that land you in the media spotlight. Imagine, if you will, the same situation described above in which you arrive at work and your lobby is filled with reporters. But instead of dread, you feel a sense of ease because you're looking into the familiar faces of reporters you've already met, had lunch with, invited to company functions, and fed good story ideas about your industry. This won't change the fact that you'll still have to answer questions, but your chances of being believed and treated fairly will increase in direct proportion to the amount of trust reporters feel with you.

Prepare in Advance for a Media Crisis

AS PART OF PLANNING FOR THE FUTURE OF YOUR BUSINESS, make an effort to meet with local reporters who cover the business beat or any other industry beats that pertain to your line of work. The effort is a prudent investment of time for three reasons, only one of which deals with crisis situations:

1 If you never experience a crisis, you will at least have established a relationship with people who can advise you on how to secure publicity.

2 Reporters might turn to you as an industry expert for quotes and insights for other stories.

3 If you ever experience a crisis, they might give you the benefit of the doubt and treat you fairly in their coverage.

The hardest thing to do in the glare of the unexpected is to step to one side and objectively look at your organization. But you will want to, because public communication about your company through the news media provides a third-party summary of your situation and your message, and with that can come implied credibility to what you're saying. A well-delivered news report can give viewers the impression that the media have looked into your affairs and that what you say must be viable. It is for this reason you need to have already done a lot of advance brainstorming and planning, especially regarding any area where you might have some media exposure. This chapter will explain what you should do during unexpected news media encounters involving questions, interviews, and visits.

Susan Gamson Karl, co-owner, president, and CEO of Annabelle Candy Company in Hayward, California, says that the news media camped in her parking lot for a week after learning that a consumer had bitten into an Annabelle's rocky-road candy bar and encountered a meal moth.

"Instead of calling us, the woman called the local TV station, and they just went nuts," Karl explains. "The first question I got from a reporter was whether or not we were going to be recalling all the candy bars. I was pretty media unsavvy then, so I responded, 'Well, not right now. We're looking into it.' And that was the truth. We were making a very serious effort to find out what had happened. But that night, to my horror, the TV station put a banner across the screen that quoted me as saying 'No, we're not pulling our product.' After that, the damage was done. The news went out on the AP wire, and we had the media in our parking lot for a week."

Karl says that the FDA did a thorough review and never did request a recall, but the media damage left Annabelle's no option. The fifty-person company recalled all its rocky-road candy, which Karl says involved millions of bars.

HEADS UP! THE MEDIA ARE ON THEIR WAY

MOST EVENTS THAT START IN-HOUSE CAN STAY IN-HOUSE, especially if the issue involves people. After all, employee problems should be handled with discretion inside the organization. However, there are times—even with employee issues—when the controversy, debate, or danger seeps outside company boundaries. Quite suddenly the company can find itself the center of media and community attention. When this happens, the best thing the company can do is to establish itself as the primary source of information about the company and the problem.

Unfortunately, a common reaction during a crisis or negative situation is to try to avoid reporters or evade their questions, which always is a risky media relations tactic. Instead of squelching curiosity, your unavailability or your evasiveness piques reporters' interest and verifies that they should persist with their stories and their line of questioning.

⟨ What to Do

Meet with the media! If fate has decided that you are in a crisis, then you're in a crisis. Accept your role and work with it. Fighting against it will only cost you time and image.

When you meet with the media, choose your words carefully. During crisis times, every statement you make should be a step in maintaining your credibility and restoring your organization's precrisis image. The best way to keep your credibility and image intact is to deal with the media in a timely, open manner, giving them candid and accurate answers.

You don't have to sacrifice company stability or personal integrity to work with the media. It is possible to be open and honest with the news media and satisfy their requests and, at the same time, get your message across and walk away unscathed. To do so, you have to do three things:

1 **Understand how the media work.** TV journalists have the tightest deadlines and need footage with good graphic appeal; radio reporters need a quiet place to audiotape you; and print journalists need lots and lots of details. But the differences don't end there, so learn all you can now about how reporters operate and put stories together.

2 **Practice bridging smoothly from the questions the news media might ask to the points that you want to make.** Remember, in most news stories, the questions are not printed or aired; only the answers are used, so make sure your answers give the information you want to give.

3 **Practice those techniques in a simulated crisis setting.** Brainstorm about the types of questions you will be asked in adverse situations. With colleagues or employees, practice putting answers together, then practice their delivery.

The bottom line in a crisis is that even if you don't talk to reporters, somebody else will: onlookers, witnesses, former employees, the competition, or unhappy customers.

Start by prioritizing your concerns about the event for the media. Let them know that public issues (Are people safe? Is everything being done to protect the community and the environment? Are you doing everything you can to safeguard employees and to end the situation?) take precedence over company issues (Will we be sued? How much will this cost in lost revenue and time? How fast can we get back to work?). In 1993, when Pepsi-Cola learned that a Seattle resident had found a syringe in a Diet Pepsi can, the company focused on safety, not on clearing its good name, even though it was innocent. The company knew that by making its primary concern the welfare of consumers, vindication would follow. And it did. The tamperings were proven to be a hoax, and Pepsi-Cola's reputation and sales recovered quickly.

CAUGHT OFF-GUARD: YOU'VE JUST LEARNED ABOUT THE SITUATION

THE EARLY STAGES OF ANY UNEXPECTED SITUATION ARE THE
most difficult and frightening because that's when your
organization has the least information and the most vulnerability. And it's at that very time when the questions from the
media—and the public—begin, especially over the phone.
Questions like these:

◆ Who's at fault?
◆ Weren't you prepared for this?
◆ Didn't you know that the sprinkler system was out of order?
◆ Didn't you know that the wind might sometimes blow from
the north, right across the materials storage area?
◆ Didn't you know that the railroad track has a speed limit of
35 mph, but that trains regularly go 45 or 50 mph?
◆ Didn't you know that your parking lot is too small for people
and pedestrians to safely maneuver simultaneously?
◆ Didn't you know that if that chemical ever exploded fifty
neighbors would have to evacuate their homes indefinitely?

These are the types of probing questions reporters will
immediately ask.

What to Do

When the unexpected hits, remember that it's OK to tell a
reporter that you don't know the answers, but that you're trying to find out. Then make sure you go after those answers
in a timely manner and get back to the reporters.

Meanwhile, it would be helpful if you could serve the
media in another way until those answers are available; for
example, provide them with background information or
summary materials. Consider preparing several prescripted
messages that emergency personnel (your employees) can
read when the signal is given. These scripts typically leave
blank lines to be filled in at the time of the emergency so that
actual descriptions of the situation can be included. Also provide employees with prepared forms and logs to record
callers' names and questions for potential callbacks.

Prepare informational materials too, including press
kits, background materials, and fact sheets discussing the

company, personnel, and safety and performance issues. Planning now to meet with the news media is important logistically also. If you have no plan, you and your employees will have to waste precious time making mundane decisions. Planning prepares solutions in advance for the logistical and administrative tasks, leaving you free to deal with the content portion of the unexpected situation.

IGNORING THE PUBLIC RELATIONS REPERCUSSIONS

MANY COMPANIES EXPERIENCING A TECHNICAL CRISIS VIEW it as a technical problem needing a technical response. They may not realize they have a public relations problem, too. If a company responds to a crisis well but fails to communicate that properly, the perception might be that the response was ineffective. As a result, the company's reputation may be tarnished, and there are few assets on a company's balance sheet worth more than its reputation (see Chapter 1).

According to research from the Institute for Crisis Management in Louisville, Kentucky, some types of crises receive more attention from the media than others. The top reason cited is the degree of controversy involved in the story. According to the institute's president, Larry Smith, "When a crisis arises from conflict between parties, a journalist will be more likely to find nonroutine news sources from which to build the stories. More sources reasonably generates more stories."

As Smith explains, the range of views about a subject is relatively uniform in nonconflict stories. "For controversial issues, though, journalists are more concerned about objectivity, which leads them to find a diverse range of voices." The research, then, suggests that any crisis involving controversy stands a greater chance of generating public relations repercussions.

 What to Do

Do not sweep the crisis under the proverbial rug in the hopes that it will blow over. The media will probably find out anyway about your negative situation, so you'd be much better off informing them proactively and explaining what happened than having them learn about it from someone else. Strategically, you have the most to lose, so you should be the one to announce your bad news first. Likewise, you should be the one to announce your defense to the media.

For example, I once had a client who used abstract sheep drawings to advertise her line of jackets and vests that she wove on her own looms. Before long, rumor spread—we think chiefly by competitors—that the pictures meant that the animals were being mistreated. Of course, the accusations were ridiculous, because my client didn't even own sheep; she purchased her wool wholesale. We decided to announce in a news release that she would discontinue using the controversial drawings because they were being misinterpreted by readers. We did this rather than waiting for others to notice that they were no longer being used because we didn't want to give the competitors the chance to gloat over a victory or claim that they had uncovered animal cruelty on the part of my client.

There's an old PR edict that when it comes to the news media during adverse times, you should "Tell it all and tell it fast." President Bill Clinton learned that too late in the Monicagate controversy. Your attorneys will probably counter that edict with one of their own: "Don't apologize, don't admit, don't tell." Remember, attorneys are paid to keep their clients out of court. In their opinion, you should not admit to anything that might cost you money later. They'll tell you, "Don't say you're sorry, or they'll get all your money if and when we go to court."

Research shows that historically, companies have recovered more quickly from negative judgments in the courtroom than from a negative judgment by the public. Thus, it's wise to be as up-front with the news media as you can. A few years ago a couple of waitresses in Minneapolis sued the Hooters restaurant chain because they said they were asked to wear tops that were too small and that when they accepted their jobs they were led to believe that Hooters had something to do with owls. The news show *Date-*

line NBC picked up the story and contacted Hooters, whose marketing department enthusiastically agreed to an interview. Why? The company rationalized that not only would they get to defend their position, but they would also have the chance to tell 20 million people for fifteen minutes on prime-time television what their restaurants are all about—an opportunity they never could have afforded otherwise. The strategy worked. By choosing public opinion over legal opinion, they set sales records in the weeks immediately following the broadcast, and the lawsuit became a nonissue.

But each situation is different, and you have to make judgments about your situation based upon the circumstances surrounding the event. For example, perhaps the concern is criminal charges against your organization. Even though the public is entitled to reasonably prompt and full disclosure of facts, your company is also entitled to the chance to build a proper defense. Or sometimes a company's insurance will be subject to a stipulation that the insurer may deny coverage if the company involved acted in a way that it eliminated the insurer's chances of successfully defending a claim arising from the crisis. So, in these cases, how do you balance disclosing facts quickly with taking the time to build a proper defense? The answer is that you do not admit any adverse information unless you are reasonably certain that the fact or opinion is accurate and is fairly treated. In other words, do not speculate. And most of all, find a happy middle ground with your legal counsel about what you can and cannot say.

EVERYTHING ABOUT AN INCIDENT SEEMS NEGATIVE

DURING A CRISIS, IT SEEMS THAT NEGATIVITY BEGETS NEGA-tivity. When all seems hopeless, it's hard to imagine that anything good could come about as a result of the misfortune. It's often at this time that I remind clients that the Chinese word for crisis is composed of two characters: danger and opportunity.

 **What to Do**

A crisis is an opportunity for you to explain to your community and the world what it is you actually do, what your business is all about, and how you go about doing that business. If you survive the potential media onslaught and endless array of questions, you might find that you and your organization are more firmly entrenched in your community and your field than before the crisis. The Hooters lawsuit I discussed in the previous example is a good illustration of seizing an opportunity to turn a crisis into a benefit.

Let's say your company stores and uses a hazardous substance. If there is a significant leak or spill, the immediate issues are: the health and safety of the community and your employees; and the perception of safety and reliability by local citizens, customers, and government officials. A secondary issue is whether or not your company will be penalized by the government. Other secondary issues include: how fast you can get back to full production, what it will take to restore operation, how quickly you can fill customers' orders and deliver their products, and how you will change your processes and procedures as a result. It is during the delivery of these secondary issues that you have tremendous opportunity to educate (and impress) the community about what it is your company does and how it does it.

YOU'RE RECEIVING UNEXPECTED INTERVIEW REQUESTS

NOT ALL INTERVIEW REQUESTS COME DURING CRISIS TIMES. During an interview you may be informed about a brewing crisis. Take some steps to control the situation.

 **What to Do**

Research the reason behind the interview request. Find out exactly who is calling, what organization the reporter represents, and why he or she wants to talk to you. If the interview request seems unusual, then ask what the reporter's deadline is and if you can get back to him or her in an hour. Then hang up the phone and think about what you want to do, or talk to a trusted employee or mentor about it.

And remember, when it comes to your business, no interview or contact with the media is too routine or too trivial. You should take every chance you get to influence the public about your product or service.

NEWS MEDIA ARE SWARMING

LIKE ANNABELLE CANDY'S CEO SUSAN KARL, MENTIONED AT the beginning of this chapter, you may find yourself inundated with news media. When this happens, and depending upon the size of your office, you may find meeting rooms, chairs, and supplies in short supply. Rather than being able to deal with the situation at hand, your efforts might be lost to taking care of administrative and logistical details.

What to Do

Review in advance which resources you have available to help you host a swarm of news media: facilities, vehicles, telephones, telephone lists, fax machines, computers, photocopy machines, lists, stationery, maps, charts, diagrams, videos, fact sheets, etc. Decide the following:

◆ Where will you meet with the media?
◆ Do you have a primary and backup location?
◆ Are the above items available twenty-four hours a day?
◆ Is backup equipment available?
◆ Do you have twenty-four-hour service agreements?
◆ Whom do you call if equipment breaks?
◆ Do you have access to twenty-four-hour printing services?
◆ Do you have a way to let employees know where the media-gathering areas are so they can direct reporters appropriately?
◆ Are the locations easily accessible?
◆ Do you have routes from all directions already written down that you can fax them to the media when an emergency hits?
◆ Does the location provide security, ample parking, electricity, eating facilities, and room for camera risers and on-camera interviews?

YOU UNEXPECTEDLY FIND YOURSELF AS SPOKESPERSON

COMMUNICATING EFFECTIVELY WITH THE NEWS MEDIA requires special skills and knowledge. It is a difficult task under the best of circumstances, and when you're dealing with highly technical and complex issues, it can be overwhelming. In an emergency, when emotions are high and definitive answers sometimes do not exist, only trained people can communicate clearly and credibly.

Sometimes you might have to disseminate messages when there is not enough relevant data or time to allow you to conduct a thorough review, and there is no time to obtain better information.

Annabelle Candy's Karl offers this advice: "Don't talk to anybody about the situation if you haven't already learned and practiced how to work with the news media. Instead, wait until you have a PR person to help you. The reason I say this is because the media took a very tiny story and almost ruined our business."

ⓒ What to Do

Training and preparation for a spokesperson should emphasize working with and relating to the media, audience analysis, message preparation and strategy, formulating effective sound bites and quotable quotes, and smoothly bridging from the reporter's question to the company's agenda. Every statement should be a step in maintaining credibility.

ⓒ What You Can Say

◆ **Prepare a concise introductory statement about the crisis.** Detail the steps you're taking to remedy the situation, and be as open as possible. Having this information ready—and being willing to share it—tells reporters that you (the spokesperson) are a viable, primary source. Although you can't tell them everything (because you don't know it or because it's proprietary information), you can give them something to work with. As a result, you'll be helping them do their story, and they'll be more likely to come back to you, instead of someone else, for more information later on.

◆ **Provide as much information and explanation as you can.** The general rule is: Tell them what you know, tell them what you don't know, and tell them what remains uncertain or ambiguous. And do it in that order. This effort shows that you are aware of the media's needs and are trying to fulfill them.

◆ **Summarize the events during each briefing you conduct.** The reporters you are addressing may not be the same ones who were in the audience during the last update, or new reporters may have just arrived.

◆ **Craft answers for the questions you will most likely receive.** Brainstorm with a colleague on what you might be asked and prepare accordingly. Practice bridging from an uncomfortable question to an answer that you want to deliver.

◆ **Provide simple and easy-to-follow explanations.** Reporters can write quickly, but they can also misquote you. So talk in simple terms. Be succinct and to the point.

◆ **Explain the approach your organization plans to take to the crisis.** List the tasks or priorities in order of importance and explain why each task has gotten its designation. Offer background and insights into the response decision making.

◆ **Dispel any rumors you receive immediately.** It may seem unwise to bring them up, but if you don't take the opportunity to correct them, they may be interpreted as fact. However, try not to use negative phrasing.

◆ **Simplify and translate numbers and technical jargon.** Explain numbers and technical situations as though you were talking to a ten-year-old child—not in a condescending manner, but with the same simplicity.

◆ **Repeat the information if at any time you think a reporter did not understand you.** However, do not insult the reporter. Instead, say: "The point that I have made is difficult; let me run through it again just to be sure I was clear and you got what you needed."

◆ **Ask the reporter questions, if necessary.** If you're not completely clear about a reporter's question, then ask for clarification. If they make statements rather than questions, ask them if they have a question.

⬤ What Not to Say

◆ **Do not be led into a trap.** Be on the lookout for ploys designed to create controversy. Instead, always bridge a negative point with a positive one.

◆ **Do not place blame in an attempt to clear your name or the name of your company.** You will come across as petty and defensive. Let the facts speak for themselves.

◆ **Don't lie.** Always tell the truth. If you don't know an answer, say so. If you say you don't know, offer follow-up if appropriate. Promise to get the information—if you're sure you can—then get the answer as soon as possible. Or if you can't provide an answer, explain why.

Bear in mind, however, that speaking the truth does not mean taking the company books out into the auditorium and passing them around. You don't have to answer every question or offer more than is asked, unless it is in your best interest. Speaking the truth means never saying anything that is not true. In an effort to be helpful, interviewees and spokespeople often suggest something that they believe is true. As a result, it gets reported as fact, and then when it's proven incorrect, the company loses all credibility with the community and the media.

Annabelle's Karl would agree. Her advice when dealing with the news media? "Stay calm, and don't try to hide anything. Always tell the truth. Be very up-front about everything that is happening. The last thing you want to do is make your situation worse by delivering inaccurate information, or worse, outright lies. We spoke the truth about our situation, and as a result, our reputation was enhanced."

◆ **Stress human compassion, but do not apologize.** This can too often be interpreted as guilt. It is possible to convey heartfelt sorrow by saying "We are saddened by" instead of "We apologize for." Express your understanding of a loss and make it clear that you and other coworkers or organization members feel the loss, too. But do not admit guilt; this will cause concern for your legal adviser, and that's not a battle you need to deal with in the heat of everything else.

Bear in mind that saying "We're sorry" is not an admission of guilt. When a crisis occurs, your company is not necessarily guilty of a crime, but you do feel bad about it. That's a big difference. And more important, that's what people want to hear initially.

When Johnson & Johnson's Tylenol capsules were tampered with by an unknown criminal, the company had every right to say it wasn't their fault. Instead, they accepted responsibility (not blame!) and didn't hide behind the problem or try to affix the blame on someone else. They presented themselves as devoting every effort to fixing the problem, not pointing fingers.

◆ **Never minimize the perceived danger or trivialize the risks.** Even when you know that the risks have been overblown, don't downplay the popular perception. Instead use facts, examples, and comparisons to deliver your message.

◆ **Never say "No comment."** The term generally implies guilt. If you have no answer and cannot comment on a question, say why, then either offer to get back to the reporter when things change or offer the reporter information of equal or better value. For example: "When the legal action is resolved, then I can answer that for you." Or, "We have not seen the report yet. When we have had time to analyze/verify/investigate it, we will have something to say. But I can tell you this ..."

◆ **Never say anything "off the record."** Nothing is ever off the record. If you don't want it printed or broadcast, don't say it. Assume there is a reporter or a microphone everywhere, even in the bathroom, the elevators, restaurants, etc. Once said, the words are reporters' property. They may not use your name, but they will say something like this: "It has been learned from other sources that ..." or "An unnamed XYZ official said ..."

◆ **Know when to elaborate and when to stop.** It is human nature to respond to questions even without the right answer or all the information for a good answer. We feel compelled to answer. However, the longer you take in responding to a question, the more likely you will later regret something you said. There is a technique reporters use called "the pregnant pause" in which the reporter stops questioning and waits for you to continue. However, after you have made your point, you are finished. Dead air is the reporter's problem. Wait out the pause or ask, "Anything else?"

◆ **Do not curse or use words in anger.** Remember that a reporter's heated words and accusations will not be shown on the six o'clock news. Instead, what will be featured is you losing your cool for no obvious reason.

◆ **Do not assume that one unscrupulous reporter represents them all.** While there will always be unscrupulous people in any line of work, most journalists—like all professionals—try to operate with ethical standards. If it seems that journalists' standards have declined in the last several years, however, it could be due to competition. In the past twenty years, the United States has gone from having three media networks to having more than thirty-five.

AN OUNCE OF PREVENTION WHEN SERIOUS INJURY OCCURS

DURING A CRISIS, YOU SHOULD PROVIDE AS MUCH INFORMA-tion to the media as you can. Being able to provide the answers before you are even asked the questions will give the media the impression that you are in tune with their information needs. This effort will help to establish trust and will keep them waiting at your location for more news rather than going behind your back to interview anyone they can find.

Below is a list of questions to review prior to giving your first (and all subsequent) briefing(s). Even if you don't have all the answers, proceed with the briefing. Instead of being able to give the media answers, you will be able to tell them that you are still investigating; then tell them the specific information you're trying to secure.

◆ **Casualties**
  — How many were injured or killed?
  — Were they employees, visitors, or outsiders?
  — How many children/visitors/innocent bystanders were involved?
  — How many were evacuated?
  — What is the nature of their injuries?
  — What care/first aid have they received?

— Where were the injured treated?

— Was anyone of prominence involved?

— Are there any accounts of people trying to escape injury? How was the escape accomplished, hindered, or stopped?

— How did the victims' families learn of the crisis?

— What will be done for the families of the victims?

◆ **Descriptions of the emergency**

— When did it happen?

— How far has the emergency spread?

— What blasts, collapses, accidents, explosions, spills, fires, releases were involved?

— What chemical/products/guns/ammunition/equipment was involved?

— What levels of chemicals/radiation/pollutants were spilled/released?

— What safety system/equipment/feature failed?

— What are the current temperature, humidity, and wind conditions, and are they favorable or unfavorable in the wake of the incident? What is the short-term forecast, and how will changes in weather affect the situation?

— Did the facility notify authorities of use and/or storage of any hazardous substance?

— Where can the media get copies of Material Safety Data Sheets (MSDSs)?

— Describe the soundness of the structures, systems, and equipment.

— What will be the next steps?

— How will this be cleaned up/corrected/improved?

— What is the total dollar amount of damage?

— What must occur for the emergency to be considered over?

◆ **Causes**

— How was the emergency discovered?

— Who sounded the alarm and summoned aid?

— What role did human error play in this emergency?

— What work/activities were being conducted at the time of the emergency?

— What are the storage conditions for any substances involved?

— Was the organization/facility aware of the risk it posed?

— What training is provided to employees?

— Can we have an account from the participants?

— Can we have an account from the witnesses?

— Can we have accounts from key responders (e.g., fire, police, FBI, Coast Guard, HazMat teams)?

◆ **Public safety/health consequences**

— What are the public health consequences?

— How would humans be exposed to any hazardous material? (Breathe it? Eat it? Absorb it through the skin?) Is the water safe to drink?

— Who are especially susceptible? Children? Seniors?

◆ **Rescue and relief**

— How many people are involved in rescue and relief operations?

— How many were evacuated from the accident site?

— How many prominent people were on the relief crew?

— What equipment was used?

— What were the impediments to rescue and obstacles to correcting the problem?

— How was the emergency prevented from spreading?

— How was property saved?

— Were there any acts of heroism?

— When will the emergency/crisis be over?

◆ **Public protection**

— What does shelter mean?

— What does evacuation mean?

— Who decides what actions the public should take?

— Where are these decision makers located?

— What are their credentials?

— How did the decision makers learn of the emergency?

— What agencies have responded to the emergency?

— What agencies are expected to respond to the emergency?

— What methods have been used to educate the general public and employees about potential emergencies at the organization/facility involved?

◆ **Property/equipment damage**

— What is the estimated value of the loss?

— Describe the kind of building or equipment involved.

— Was any other property threatened?

— Describe previous emergencies or past problems with this equipment.

◆ **Legal actions**

— How will the emergency affect your stock price and financial standing?

— Will this cause real estate values in the area to decrease?

— How much insurance is available, and from where?

◆ **Heroes and culprits.** Be prepared for the media to request interviews. They'll want names, addresses, phone numbers, etc. Decide in advance how to respond.

◆ **Witnesses, experts, and company VIPs.** Be prepared for the media to request interviews. Be prepared to provide contact information for those who are available and explanations for why the others are not available.

KEY AUDIENCES ARE HEARING ABOUT YOUR CRISIS FROM SOMEONE ELSE

WHEN AN UNEXPECTED SITUATION HAPPENS, CERTAIN PEOPLE associated with your organization will think they should have been notified immediately and in person, but certainly not with the rest of the world by the news media.

What to Do

In any far-reaching crisis, the news media are your primary communication device to reach the broad public. But the mistake companies often make is that they depend solely on the media to communicate with the key audiences they need to talk to.

Determine now: How would a crisis and your reaction to it be interpreted by everyone whom you try to inform or persuade? How can you communicate with them during a crisis so that you do not undo the good you already have done with them? How would these audiences want to be informed?

Many companies conduct spokesperson training and think they have prepared adequately for the public information aspects of an emergency. Don't fall into that trap. The media are not the only audience you must reach. You have many other audiences that need to be addressed in your planning, according to R. Matt Davis, who formerly worked with public affairs at Dow Chemical Company's Midland, Michigan, facility. Following a CSX train derailment in 1989, chemicals from several companies, including Dow, were spilled, prompting the evacuation of almost 1,000 people from their homes for a week.

Davis recalls, "The emergency wasn't isolated to the incident itself; few emergencies are. There's always a lot of commotion and activity on the side that demands your attention, and for which too many companies fail to plan. We had emergency responders going in to deal with the spill, evacuated residents trying to obtain lodging and settle up with the train company, media and elected officials requesting tours of the incident site, residents forming community forums on the side, the Coast Guard flying over the derailment site trying to identify all problem areas, and police cordoning off access roads. On top of that, another train which carries products to our facility uses the same track as the train that derailed," Davis continues. "That brings up another complication when an incident happens: How do you keep operations going at your facility, keep people safe, and not have to shut down your plant? And you have to make sure your other various audiences—suppliers, vendors, stockholders—know the status of your company."

Should a negative event happen, make a special effort to contact key company players and supporters to let them know how you plan to rectify the situation.

NEWS MEDIA ARE REPORTING INACCURATE INFORMATION

SOMETIMES, DESPITE YOUR BEST EFFORT TO PROVIDE FACTUAL information, the details get confused or the reporter's interpretation is incorrect. When this happens, the public hears a misleading, and sometimes damaging, story.

Your response should include a media monitoring program to ensure that what the media report is correct. You will want to audit what is being said to ensure that the public is being told the details they need to know (if public safety is in jeopardy, for example). This effort can be as simple as soliciting the help of friends and employees to watch and listen to the news and clip articles from the paper. If time and money are on your side, then contract the services of a clipping service and/or a public relations firm.

RUMORS ARE SURFACING

IF, AS EXPLAINED ABOVE, THE MEDIA DO REPORT INACCURATE information, rumors may be the result. Other times, rumors can start without the media's help. Most responsible business people have a hard time understanding how far a baseless claim or accusation can travel. Plan now how you will respond to questions from the public.

What to Do

◆ Train your switchboard operators how to handle emergency calls and where to forward them.

◆ Set up a toll-free hot line and advertise its availability. This can be as simple as contacting your telephone company and making a request, then making the news media aware of the number. A hot line is a good way for an organization to let the public know it has nothing to hide. This action also tells them you care about their concerns and you want to be accessible to them.

◆ Have people properly trained to handle phone calls. Simply reading a statement is not sufficient. During an emergency, your office and company may receive hundreds of calls. Be sure your employees know what they can and can't talk about.

YOU'RE PULLED INTO SOMEONE ELSE'S CRISIS

YOU CONDUCT YOUR OPERATIONS WELL AND PRACTICE HONESTY in every aspect of your business, unlike a competitor on the other side of town. So when that competitor is reported to be cheating customers, you feel as though justice has won out—until you realize that you are "guilty by association." If you're a funeral home director, for example, and your competitor has been accused of charging grieving customers for items and services they didn't receive, then all funeral homes in your area are subject to scrutiny, including you. The situation may be someone else's crisis, but it's *your* problem.

"Guilt by association" also develops within industries as a whole. We've seen it happen within the auto, tobacco, and apple-growing industries as a result of changing market conditions, environmental concerns, even federal involvement. For example, before President Clinton took office and attempted to "reform" health care, the health industry had an image of competency. Now that image is damaged in the eyes of the public.

What to Do

When you see your company's or industry's image becoming tarnished, take immediate action. Let the news media know that you will talk to them if they want to do a story. Update your employees and encourage them to tell the true facts to their friends and neighbors. Let the media know how you differ from the competition (without bad-mouthing your competitors, of course) or from the rest of the industry. Take a stance that will build your credibility.

The business owner of a floral design store near where I live did just that. The owner of Flowers by Jim made national headlines in 1998 when he announced to the local paper that he would be closed on Valentine's Day because he objected to certain practices within the floral industry during that time of year. It seems that wholesalers charge exorbitant prices for flowers during this holiday. He did not like charging almost double for the same bouquet of flowers on Valentine's Day that he charged on any other day. His refusal to play the game the way other florists played it came across as a personal sacrifice, on his busiest day of the year, for the good of his customers. His unconventional tactic paid off, and his reputation soared in town. Sure, this may not be a situation of crisis proportions, but it is an example of taking action to protect an intact reputation.

Another option is to adopt a team approach to combat the adversity. When the 1996 Summer Olympics were scheduled to be held in Atlanta, one apartment building owner issued a letter saying that he wasn't going to renew several leases of current tenants until after a two- to three-week vacancy. Obviously, he hoped to make a small fortune by offering lodging to out-of-town guests. Unfortunately, the news was picked up by the local media and spread to the national outlets, and the result was that all apartment owners in Atlanta felt the negativity. One owner pulled together other landlords to establish a policy through the Atlanta Apartment Association that all apartment owners would behave responsibly. The controversy died quickly after that.

YOU'RE TEMPTED TO STRIKE BACK WHEN YOU FEEL DAMAGED

DESPITE YOUR BEST EFFORTS AT ACCOMMODATING THE NEWS media, you might get the impression that they're out to deliver a sensationalized story no matter how straightforward and cooperative you are. When this happens, the urge to strike back with paid advertisements, handouts, or other tactics can be strong.

Likewise, it often seems that journalists target business-people as villains. This is, in part, true, according to a 1997 Media Research Center study, which suggested that journalists are simply confirming existing prejudices that are revealed in the entertainment industry. A study of prime-time network television for more than two years, including more than 800 TV shows and movies, showed that TV businessmen are shown committing crimes more often than those in any other occupation. Of the criminals portrayed, 29.2 percent were business executives, while only 9.7 percent were career criminals and 3.9 percent were government officials.

What to Do

As a small-company owner, your best strategy when you feel like striking back at the news media is to go into a closed room and yell. Fighting the media at their own game is for the big guys, and even then, its effectiveness is debated among public relations and legal experts. Most often, an attempt to set the public straight just draws more attention to a story that otherwise would have gone unnoticed by most people, leaving your company worse off than if you had left bad enough alone.

For example, when Metabolife International was interviewed by ABC's 20/20 in 1999 regarding a customer's claim to have been damaged by its diet pills, the company posted on the Internet its own copy of the full video of the interview before the 20/20 airing. Metabolife's management believed that there generally is no achievable justice after a story has aired, so it wanted to be the one that brought the story to the attention of the public first. However, some communications experts argue that all Metabolife did was to draw more attention to a negative situation.

Additionally, a small company is dependent upon the local media. Anger them, and you'll be their target for years to come. In contrast, when big companies fight back in the national news media, they're not dealing with the only media available to them. They can pursue a clean-up campaign through their local media outlets. But if you're a small company that has secured the wrath of the locals, where can you turn? Generally, you can't move up to national media attention for your retaliatory campaign.

Bottom line: When you feel attacked, your best bet is to reread this chapter, maintain your composure, and weather the storm. Carefully analyze why you have been targeted for notoriety, and correct any negative traits that you can. Be as open and up-front as you can be with the media and let your reputation win out through time against a media smear. Now, if it is obvious that not defending yourself makes you look guilty as opposed to defensive, then the rules for response may change. See the following entry.

And finally, establish a relationship and a rapport with the news media for the purpose of good and responsible day-to-day management. After all, the media are a means by which to reach your customers during good times as well as bad.

Words and Phrases to Avoid with the News Media

- abandon
- accidents happen
- benefits outweigh risks
- catastrophe
- code blue
- condition red
- crisis
- dead end
- delay
- despair
- disaster
- don't worry
- doom
- everyone's worried about nothing
- everything carries risk
- failure
- fate
- give up
- hide
- hopeless
- I already told you that once
- inconsequential
- inconsolable
- inexcusable
- inexplicable
- incomprehensible
- insignificant
- it's the media's fault
- it will only impact a few or a small population
- limitations
- lost control
- meaningless
- mistake
- (anything that implies) my information is better than yours
- no comment
- not my problem
- out of control
- out of our hands now
- panic
- quit
- ridiculous
- scramble
- screw-up
- shameful
- S.O.S.
- this is off the record
- tragedy
- trivial
- trust me, trust us, we're the experts
- unimportant
- unlucky
- waste
- we know what we're doing
- we're innocent
- we're not to blame
- we're not responsible
- we're only human
- we're under no obligation to discuss that
- you don't understand
- you weren't listening

YOU NEED TO STRIKE BACK WHEN SOMEONE HAS DONE YOU DAMAGE

IN SOME SITUATIONS, IN CONTRAST TO THE SCENARIO described above, you may have to strike back, because not doing so would imply guilt. This situation can work if your foe is someone other than the news media and the media are looking to you to respond and defend yourself. Doing so does not give your enemy credibility; instead, it shows that you believe yourself innocent of the accusations and want to set the record straight.

What to Do

Make sure that you're not fighting back needlessly. If the accusations have no merit, are not being taken seriously by media or the public, and seem to be dying a quick death, then you may want to drop the issue. To fight it would just bring more unnecessary attention to it, thereby giving it more legs and credibility than it merits.

Also determine whether you can afford the repercussions of a fight. I have seen companies fight unfounded accusations and cause such a stir from the retaliatory effort that government investigators had to make an appearance to save face. The result was a hefty fine for other problems the investigators discovered while there, whereas the original accusations proved to have no merit.

217

The Bottom Line

FROM BLUE MOUNTAIN PUBLISHING TO PEPSI TO KATHIE LEE Giffords's clothing line, businesses are finding themselves the top story of the day or in the headline above the fold, thanks to news media, headline-seekers, disgruntled employees, and others whose motives are not always clear. If this happens to you, then reread this chapter and reduce the damage. Meanwhile, follow the advice that you can right now, so that you can avoid getting nailed in the first place.

Resources

Collecting Supportive Data

COLLECTING DATA ON LIKELY CRISES, YOUR AUDIENCE, AND
your competition is smart business, if you do it before a crisis hits, when you have time to analyze and use the information. Here are three sites that will help you in your search.
You'll find more sites for checking on your competition in
the following category, Competitive Sleuthing.

◆ **Institute for Crisis Management (www.crisisexperts.com).**
If you can ignore the slow loading and confusing home page,
this Kentucky-based organization's site offers an extensive
list of books and articles on crisis management and news
you might want to review. It also has a database of more than
60,000 business-crisis news stories for the past ten-plus
years. For a fee, you can get specialty searches through this
database when you're looking for specifics on a particular
type of crisis.

◆ **Intellectual Property Network (patents.ibm.com).** Want
to know what products your competition has been producing? Search by individual or company in this large patent
database, sponsored by IBM, to get the scoop on new inven-
tions. According to IBM, the site was developed for internal
use, but the company quickly recognized the demand for a
user-friendly patent database—and, no doubt, the potential
for publicity and profit. Search the database by simple key-
word, patent number, Boolean text, or multiple text fields.
You can even search for patents in Europe and Japan. Best
of all, you can just browse through the lists if you like. All
collections are cross-referenced and forward and backward
linked to all other referencing documents for immediate
access to related information.

◆ **U.S. Census Bureau (www.census.gov).** The first rule in
avoiding costly marketing mistakes is to know who your
audience is and what they want. This site is a treasure chest
of demographic and statistical information on the people of
the United States.

Competitive Sleuthing

IT'S SMART BUSINESS TO STAY ABREAST OF WHAT YOUR COMPE-
tition is doing. Besides visiting their offices and stores occa-
sionally and reviewing their marketing materials, you should
look them up on these sites.

◆ **Hoover's Online (www.hoovers.com).** Touts itself as the
Web's most comprehensive source of business information,
including intelligence, products, and services. Research the
competition at this site using drop-down search boxes on
every page. You can also perform a sitewide search that
includes results from all of Hoover's Online's features,
including company and industry information, news, features, and directories. There's free information and free
newsletters, although some reports have price tags. Members get more benefits.

◆ **Company Sleuth (www.companysleuth.com).** If you want
to monitor a competitor, try this: Type in the names of up to
ten public companies, and it'll track news, stock prices, ana-
lyst reports, and much more, giving you personalized daily
updates via e-mail and on your personal digital assistant.
Best of all, it's free. You'll also get special e-mail alerts when
big news about those companies breaks. Also access stock
quotes, news, insider trades, domain names, trademarks and
patent registrations, and message boards. The home page
alone features the "Top Ten Companies Being Watched" and
"Top Ten Stakeouts Requested."

◆ **Venture Capital Survey
(dbserv.mercurycenter.com/business/moneytree/).** Want
to know what companies in your industry have been dip-
ping into venture capitalists' pockets? This database can
probably tell you. The data are compiled from a Mercury
News/PricewaterhouseCoopers LLP survey of venture capitalists nationwide to find out whose accounts their funds
are filling. Private funding is not reported, so the listings
aren't comprehensive. Simply search by year, quarter,
industry type, company name, and amount of funding.
This site provides a list of companies, how much they got,
and from whom.

◆ **KnowX.com (www.knowx.com).** This engine searches public records and—for about $1 to $5 in most cases—will report on bankruptcies, liens, judgments, and such against both individuals and businesses. Check it out so that you know what you're getting into before you enter business agreements, choose service providers, or make other costly investments.

◆ **CreditFYI.com (www.creditfyi.com).** Just $14.95 will buy you a credit report, delivered in seconds, on a small business with $5 million or less in sales. You get a simple one-screen summary of the small business's credit history and a risk rating that evaluates its relative likelihood of paying bills on time.

Consultants Offering Free Information

FORTUNATELY, A COMMON PRACTICE ON THE WEB THESE DAYS is to give away helpful information in the hopes that visitors will appreciate it so much that they'll come back for more business or buy a book. These four sites have adopted this practice: You can read their articles for free, without obligation. But be forewarned: they are all consultants or authors hoping to sell to you. I mention the sites not to endorse their owners but to make you aware of some more opinions and free advice.

◆ **Rothstein Catalog on Disaster Recovery by Rothstein Associates (www.rothstein.com/features.html).** Articles range from computer viruses to slow-motion disaster.

◆ **"All Hazards" Crisis Management Planning (palimpsest.stanford.edu/byauth/sikich/allhz.html).** An article with the premise that accidents don't make appointments. They can occur anytime and under the most unfavorable circumstances.

◆ **Crisis Management—Excerpts from *Winning with the News Media* (www.winning-newsmedia.com/crisis.htm).** This article, "The First Hours Are Critical in Avoiding Damage or Death," is made up of excerpts from the book.

◆ **Wilson Group Communications (www.wilson-group.com/).** Articles range from dealing with the media and PR repercussions to training and management issues.

Employee Concerns

WITH EMPLOYEES CAN COME A HOST OF POTENTIAL PROBLEMS and concerns for any small business. Seek out the right information and hire the right people now for the longevity of your company.

◆ **Background Research International (www.investigator.com/lb.htm).** It's always a risk to hire new employees, because you never know what their presence will do for (or to!) your company. What's even more worrisome is what they may have done in the past. This site will tell you about the personal histories of new hires, but a search will cost you, from $75 to more than $500.

◆ **OSHA (www.osha.gov).** Find the latest employee safety and health information from the Department of Labor's Occupational Safety and Health Administration. The site features updates on legislation, news releases, contact information, a handy site search, and more. If you're looking for the booklet mentioned earlier in this book, "Consultation Services for the Employer" (OSHA publication #3047), then call or write to: OSHA Office of Information & Consumer Affairs, Room N3637, U.S. Department of Labor, Washington, DC 20210, 202-219-8151. To find an agency offering the program in your state, contact OSHA at 202-693-2213 or www.osha.gov.

◆ **Monster.com (www.monster.com).** This is probably the biggest online help-wanted site you'll find. On the day I visited, there were 376,341 listings for job hunters to review, so you know that this is where quality candidates will look periodically when job searching, and even when they're happy with their current jobs. Post your available jobs here. As a member, you also receive special benefits.

◆ **Hotjobs.com (hotjobs.com).** This site is positioning itself as a fast-rising competitor for help-wanted ads. Its description says that its "suite of services leverages the Internet to provide a direct exchange of information between job seekers and employers. We developed these services based on our experience in the recruiting industry and our in-depth understanding of the needs of job seekers and employers."

- **Free Agent (www.freeagent.com).** This is the marketplace for linking businesses with self-employed independent contractors. Knowledge of this site will come in handy when you experience a crisis or fast growth and want to hire professionals without bearing the burdens of full-time employees.
- **Guru.com (guru.com).** This is another marketplace for finding independent contractors, listing more than 170,000 gurus. Like the others, it features a handy search option.

FEMA Guidance for Free

THE FEDERAL EMERGENCY MANAGEMENT AGENCY IS A STORE-house of information on emergencies and disasters. Although its chief purpose is to provide assistance to private citizens during times of threat and crisis, it recognizes a link between commerce and recovery during adverse times. As a result, FEMA offers lots of free information developed specifically for businesses.

- *FEMA Handbook: Business Resumption Planning: A Guide* **(www.fema.gov/library/bizindex.htm).** A step-by-step approach to emergency planning, response, and recovery for companies of all sizes. Sponsored by a Public-Private Partnership with the Federal Emergency Management Agency. This booklet is intended as a brief introduction to the concept of business resumption planning and provides suggestions and guidelines on how to go about preparing a business resumption plan tailored to the needs of virtually any business or organization. Note, however, that no reporting requirements are listed, nor will following these principles ensure compliance with any federal, state, or local codes or regulations that may apply to your business. At the Web site listed, you will find a copy in PDF format to download and a Table of Contents.

The following publications can be obtained from FEMA by writing to: FEMA Publications, P.O. Box 70274, Washington, DC 20024.

- *Disaster Mitigation Guide for Business and Industry* (FEMA 190). Technical planning information for building owners and industrial facilities on how to reduce the impact of natural disasters and man-made emergencies.

◆ **Principal Threats Facing Communities and Local Emergency Management Coordinators** (FEMA 191). Statistics and analyses of U.S. natural disasters and man-made threats.

◆ **Floodproofing Non-Residential Structures** (FEMA 102). Technical information for building owners, designers, and contractors on flood prevention techniques (200 pages).

◆ **Non-Residential Flood-proofing—Requirements and Certification for Buildings Located in Flood Hazard Areas in Accordance with the National Flood Insurance Program** (FIA-TB-3). Includes planning and engineering considerations for preventing floods in new commercial buildings.

◆ **Building Performance: Hurricane Andrew in Florida** (FIA 22). Techniques for enhancing the performance of buildings in hurricanes.

◆ **Building Performance: Hurricane Iniki in Hawaii** (FIA 23). Technical guidance for reducing hurricane and flood damage.

◆ **Answers to Questions About Substantially Damaged Buildings** (FEMA 213). Information about regulations and policies of the National Flood Insurance Program regarding substantially damaged buildings.

◆ **Design Guidelines for Flood Damage Reduction** (FEMA 15). A study on land use, watershed management, design, and construction practices in flood-prone areas.

◆ **Comprehensive Earthquake Preparedness Planning Guidelines: Corporate** (FEMA 71). Earthquake planning guidance for corporate safety officers and managers.

Management

RECALL THAT IN CHAPTER 1, THE INSTITUTE FOR CRISIS MANagement reported that 75 percent of business crises could be attributed directly or indirectly to management. If you have any doubts about your management decisions but can't afford to hire professional help, then seek some free assistance. Here are several places to start.

◆ **Free Management Library (www.mapnp.org/library/crisis/crisis.htm).** This site describes itself as a "complete, highly integrated library of resources for nonprofit and for-profit businesses," but I include it here because it offers several articles on various aspects of crisis management. The overall goal of the library is to provide basic, how-to management information to managers—particularly those with very limited resources.

◆ **Smart Business Supersite (www.smartbiz.com).** News, tips, and everything else you need to start, grow, and—most pertinent to this book—protect a business. It's a good site with minimal graphics, easy navigation, and good content.

◆ **Entrepreneur.com (www.entrepreneur.com).** The archive of *Entrepreneur* magazine articles goes back to 1991. You can also post questions and search by topic.

◆ **Better Business Bureau (www.bbb.org).** If you thought this site was just for consumers, think again. Here's some of the heads-up and business protection material you'll find at the site: guidelines for ethical advertising practices, information about scams and schemes aimed at businesses, tips for merchants accepting personal checks, and advice on applying for its online privacy seal for your site.

◆ **BizMove.com (www.bizmove.com).** Self-described as the Small Business Knowledge Base, this site has hundreds of pages of practical information on prevention and protection topics such as personnel audits, cash flow management, marketing plans, and reducing costs.

Professional Help

SEEKING OUT THE BEST LEGAL, FINANCIAL, INSURANCE, AND management advice you can afford makes good sense when it comes to safeguarding your business. Start with these sites.

◆ **Attorney Find (www.attorney-find.net).** Search through possible lawyers by location and specialty, then get links to their Web sites so you can check them out before calling.

◆ **Lawyers.com (www.lawyers.com).** This site will make the old joke about too many lawyers ring true. Here you'll find information on more than 420,000 of them. Searches can be done by name, practice area, location, and more.

◆ **CPA finder (www.cpafinder.com).** Indicate the type of accountant you want and where you are, and this engine will point you to local CPAs. The site is user-friendly and features search options.

◆ **Accountant-Search (www.accountant-search.com).** More than 100,000 accountants are registered here, and searches can be done by location or specialty.

◆ **Quicken Insure/Market/Small Business Insurance (www.insuremarket.com/products/small_business/index_sb.htm).** A good place to visit to collect background on business owners' policies and workers' comp insurance.

◆ **Insurance Industry Internet Network (www.iiin.com).** Here you'll find links to more than 900 insurance companies and 700 brokers/agents. This is not an endorsement, however, so comparison shop for agents and policies.

◆ **SCORE (www.score.org).** The Service Corps of Retired Executives, a resource partner with the Small Business Administration, is a nonprofit association of more than 12,000 retired executives that offers free counseling to small businesses. You'll find how-to information, links to sites with business information, and a map to help you find a local SCORE chapter. You can get business advice via e-mail by selecting from a list of skills to find an appropriate counselor.

Publications

◆ *Disaster Recovery Journal.* The *Disaster Recovery Journal* is the first publication dedicated to the field of disaster recovery and business continuity. The first issue of the magazine was 22 pages long and was distributed to 3,000 people. Today there are well over 50,000 subscribers, and it is over 100 pages in length. Best advice: Skim the articles for practical tips—most of them were written by vendors and consultants hoping to sell their services. For subscription information, write to P.O. Box 510110, St. Louis, MO 63151, call 314-894-0276, or send a fax to 314-894-7474.

◆ *Emergency Preparedness News* **(www.bpinews.com/hs/pages/epn.htm).** Published every other week by Business Publishers, Inc., this newsletter takes you beyond the headlines of major stories and behind the scenes to show you how emergency personnel and relief officials handled an incident and what tools aided their response and recovery efforts. The subscription fee seems high, but it's not when you consider what you get for that fee. For information, write to Business Publishers, Inc., 8737 Colesville Road, Suite 1100, Silver Springs, MD 20910-3928, or call 800-274-6737.

Purchasing

THERE ARE HUNDREDS OF SITES AND BRICK-AND-MORTAR locations where you can shop for the supplies you'll need before and during a crisis. It would be impossible to include all of them, so I've included only two: one company tells you about the reliability and legitimacy of any online merchant you're considering buying from and the other is about ... well, batteries. In my experience, a crisis and batteries go together like a horse and carriage.

◆ **1-800-Batteries (www.1800batteries.com).** If you rely on a battery-powered device, you will find replacements here, because they stock many hard-to-find batteries. You'll find batteries for your most-used equipment too: cell phones, notebook PCs, specialty handheld devices, and more. They also sell related equipment, such as AC adapters, auto and in-flight adapters, and docking units.

◆ **BizRate.com (www.bizrate.com).** Take the worries out of shopping online. Type in the name of the online merchant you want to buy from and BizRate will tell you how past customers rate the sites and the service. Merchants get an overall rating; detailed ratings are also offered in ten categories, including selection, price, on-time delivery, ease of ordering, and customer support.

Safeguard Your Domain Name

SEE CHAPTER 5 ABOUT PROTECTING YOUR WEB PRESENCE.

◆ **InterNIC (www.internic.net).** This is the place to check on the availability of domain names and, likewise, the place to register the name you want for your Web site. The site is hosted by Network Solutions, Inc., on behalf of the U.S. Department of Commerce.

Searching for Money

AS WAS STATED EARLIER IN THE BOOK, YOU SHOULD ESTABLISH a relationship with your local lending institutions now so that you have access to funds when the need—or an emergency—arises. If loans make you shudder and you think you can attract investors, then start looking now. However, if those contacts just aren't working for you, here are two other places to look:

◆ **SBA Disaster Assistance (www.sbaonline.sba.gov/disaster/).** The purpose of the SBA's Disaster Loan Program is to offer financial assistance to those who are trying to rebuild their businesses (and homes) in the aftermath of a disaster. By offering low-interest loans, the SBA helps to aid long-term recovery efforts. The agency commits to doing everything possible to meet the needs of those otherwise unable to put their lives back together.

◆ **Capital Connection (www.capital-connection.com).** A clearinghouse for capital, helping entrepreneurs find capital and investors find suitable companies. This site also offers lots of guidance on dealing with venture capital and business financing issues.

Troubleshooting Computer and Internet Problems

◆ **AntiVirus Research Center (www.symantec.com/avcenter/index.html).** A comprehensive information storehouse about computer viruses. The site is sponsored by Symantec, the maker of the Norton AntiVirus programs. You'll find a series of live chat options and online tutorials. When I visited, the home page clearly listed links to descriptions of the "Top Threats."

◆ **BugNet (www.bugnet.com).** Since 1994, BugNet has delivered information on PC software bugs, alerting visitors to glitches, analyzing software trends, and compiling a comprehensive database of computer bug fixes. Each month BugNet subscribers receive more than 300 bug warnings. Warning: It's a subscription site, but there are plenty of freebies available too. When I visited the site, these two headlines featured updated information for visitors for free, along with a long list of bug alert postings: "Special: Top 30 Tax Software Bug Fixes" and "BugNet Top 10 Bug Fixes."

◆ **Internet Fraud Complaint Center (www.ifccfbi.gov/).** The FBI and the Virginia-based National White Collar Crime Center have created this site to field complaints from Net users who believe they have been victims of online fraud, cyber scams, and theft. The site contains a form you can use to file a complaint. This, in turn, alerts authorities of a suspected criminal or civil violation.

◆ **ZDNet (www.zdnet.com).** From *MacWorld* to *PC Computing*, all the magazines from the biggest publisher of tech periodicals are online, with troubleshooting tips and more. I like the link called "Help & How-To," which offers updates under such titles as Tips & Tricks, How-to, Fix It Now, and Virus Alerts & Solutions. Two articles featured the day I visited were "What is a fire wall?" and "PC Security Basics."

HOAXES

THESE ARE PLACES TO CHECK FOR INTERNET HOAXES:

◆ **http://ciac.llnl.gov/ciac/CIACHoaxes.html.** Sponsored by the Department of Energy.

◆ **www.nonprofit.net/hoax/hoax.html.** Sponsored by a private citizen.

◆ **www.symantec.com/avcenter/hoax.html.** Offered by Symantec, a world leader in Internet security technology.

◆ **http://urbanlegends.about.com/culture/urb.** This site, featured by About.com, is devoted to urban legends and folklore, but seems to specialize in seeking out the truth regarding rumors passed universally through e-mail.

Index

235

About Bloomberg

Bloomberg L.P., founded in 1981, is a global information services, news, and media company. Headquartered in New York, the company has nine sales offices, two data centers, and 79 news bureaus worldwide.

Bloomberg, serving customers in 100 countries around the world, holds a unique position within the financial services industry by providing an unparalleled range of features in a single package known as the BLOOMBERG PROFESSIONAL™ service. By addressing the demand for investment performance and efficiency through an exceptional combination of information, analytic, electronic trading, and Straight Through Processing tools, Bloomberg has built a worldwide customer base of corporations, issuers, financial intermediaries, and institutional investors.

BLOOMBERG NEWS℠, founded in 1990, provides stories and columns on business, general news, politics, and sports to leading newspapers and magazines throughout the world. BLOOMBERG TELEVISION®, a 24-hour business and financial news network, is produced and distributed globally in seven different languages. BLOOMBERG RADIO™ is an international radio network anchored by flagship station BLOOMBERG® WBBR 1130 in New York.

In addition to the BLOOMBERG PRESS® line of books, Bloomberg publishes *BLOOMBERG® MARKETS, BLOOMBERG PERSONAL FINANCE™,* and *BLOOMBERG® WEALTH MANAGER.* To learn more about Bloomberg, call a sales representative at:

Frankfurt: 49-69-92041-200	São Paulo:..........5511-3048-4530
Hong Kong: 85-2-2977-6600	Singapore: 65-212-1200
London: 44-20-7330-7500	Sydney: 61-2-9777-8601
New York: 1-212-318-2200	Tokyo:...............81-3-3201-8950
San Francisco: 1-415-912-2980	

For in-depth market information and news, visit BLOOMBERG.COM®, which draws from the news and power of the BLOOMBERG PROFESSIONAL™ service and Bloomberg's host of media products to provide high-quality news and information in multiple languages on stocks, bonds, currencies, and commodities, at **www.bloomberg.com.**

About the Author

Debra Koontz Traverso, M.A., has consulted with organizations of all sizes, from sole proprietorships to NASA to UPS, in the field of crisis management and emergency preparedness. She is a speaker, trainer, business journalist, marketing communications specialist, business owner, and member of the adjunct faculty at Harvard University. Through her company WriteDirections.com she has also worked as a writing coach and marketing consultant for both individuals and major corporations. Ms. Traverso is the author of *Outsmarting Goliath: How to Achieve Equal Footing with Companies That Are Bigger, Richer, Older, and Better Known* (Bloomberg Press, 2000), which was named *Book Sense 76* Top Ten Pick for July/August 2000. She lives in the Washington, D.C. area.